FIFTY STATES, FIFTY STORIES

FIFTY STATES, FIFTY STORIES...

I Never Thought I'd Live Here

by Lynn S. Rosenberg

Palmetto Publishing Group
Charleston, SC

First Edition

Printed in the United States

ISBN-13: 978-1-64990-109-5
ISBN-10: 1-64990-109-7

To my mother, Natalie.
She was my best friend and greatest advocate.

> If there is a book that you want to read but it hasn't been written yet, you must be the one to write it.
> —*Toni Morrison*

In the early years of living in Las Vegas, I was thrilled to see such a diversity of people. I was raised on Long Island, New York, and spent the first fifty years of my life there as a student, young bride, mother, and teacher, as did almost all of my friends and acquaintances. So after we moved to Nevada, I talked to people about how and why they came to live in Las Vegas, and I found out the reasons were varied, as you will see. However, the tagline was always the same: "I never thought I would live here!"

After hearing this common ending to almost every story, I decided that there was a book to be written about this very idea, and many stories to be told. So before anyone else ran with my idea, I decided I would be the one to write it!

I, too, never would have believed that I'd end up living in Las Vegas, based on my misconception of what this city really was about. People I interviewed talked about the great weather, access to beautiful natural parks, great food, and world-class entertainment. Few of them indicated that gambling was the stimulus that brought them here to live, contrary to the city's reputation.

Please read and enjoy these real stories collected over time from real people who ended up living in a city that they never expected to call home.

Lynn S. Rosenberg
September 2019

Some interesting facts about Las Vegas excerpted from *Las Vegas Review Journal,* article entitled "Nevada's Speed of Growth Puts Silver State Natives in Vast Minority," by Michael Scott Davidson, January 25, 2019.

- The 2017 census indicated that only 26 percent of the state's three million residents were born here. That is the smallest percentage of any state in the United States!

- During the Great Recession of 2008, thousands left Las Vegas due to the battered economy.

- From 2013 to 2017, 650,000 people moved into Las Vegas and 490,000 moved out. Former Florida residents led the influx, while former Arizonans led the migration away from Las Vegas.

- Californians are the largest group moving here. They cite less traffic, less expensive housing, and the cost of living in Las Vegas compared to California as reasons for the move. They can "live twice as well for half price."

- Robert Lang, the executive director of Brookings Mountain West at the University of Nevada, Las Vegas, says, "Southern Nevada is built by and for outsiders."

- Among newcomers, 61 percent were under the age of forty, with 30 percent having college degrees. Among people already living here under the age of forty, 53 percent hold college degrees.

- Images of the 1957 winner of the Miss Atomic Bomb beauty contest became among the most publicized photographs ever used to publicize Las Vegas. In those days, nearby nuclear testing was thought to attract tourism instead of repel it!

Many celebrity weddings have taken place in Las Vegas over the past half century:

- Mickey Rooney was noted for marrying multiple times in local wedding chapels while he was a popular movie star.

- Elvis Presley and Priscilla Beaulieu were married at the Aladdin in 1967.

- Arlene Dahl, who was married four times, famously married handsome leading man Fernando Lamas in 1954 at the Last Frontier Resort.

- Paul Newman and Joanne Woodward wed at the El Rancho in 1958.

- Bing Crosby, fifty-three, married Kathy Grant, a twenty-three-year-old starlet in 1957, after dating her for five years, at St. Anne Catholic Church.

- Zsa Zsa Gabor married actor George Sands in 1949 at the Little Church of the West, now considered a historical landmark.

The beginning was at the end of a 3,600-mile family car trip in the southwestern part of the country. We lived in New York at the time, and my then husband, our two young sons, and I flew to Denver, rented a car, and explored ten states, including all the requisite national parks. So, on the last night of this marvelous trip, the teacher in me had everyone in the family rate our experiences from one to one hundred, one being the best and one hundred being the worst. Las Vegas came in with a whopping score of ninety-seven—close to the worst!

That was 1985, and due to circumstances presented to me (I got a job as an assistant principal), I moved here in 1999. It was the last place on earth I expected to live! Once I got here, I loved the fact that people came from everywhere and had a variety of reasons for moving here. But nearly every story I heard ended with, "But I never thought I would live in Las Vegas."

I'll Start with My Story

After the death of my first husband, Gary, I remarried in 1988 to a man who was very open minded and not fixed on a life remaining on Long Island, New York. Our children were out of high school and college, so our decision was really based on just the two of us.

My dad was a businessman, always looking for the next opportunity in life, and in 1993 he owned several California Closet franchises back east. He wanted to relocate to a place that would be tax friendly and provide warm weather for golf and outdoor activities. Much to my dismay, he called me one day and said that he was moving to Las Vegas to open a closet company—as simple as that! I was in disbelief that he would move so far away from New York and to Sin City of all places! We had neither family nor friends in Las Vegas. What was wrong with my dad?

In the beginning, when we'd visit my dad in Las Vegas, he would pick us up at the airport, and on the drive to his home, he would point out all the new hotels, the glitter and the glitz that made him proud to live here. I tried to be polite and smile and feign enthusiasm, but in reality I thought the strip was way overdone for my taste and completely lacking any class.

One morning, on Long Island, in the dead of winter, I was pulling out of my garage in seventeen-degree weather. I was wearing a fur coat, driving down my block as the sleet was falling, and the defroster wasn't working yet. It was at that moment that I said to myself, "I don't want to do this anymore!" When I returned home from work that evening after enduring traffic, snowy roads, and freezing cold, I said to my husband, Ron, "Let's move. What do you think?"

Fast-forward about two years. My husband and I visited the southwest often: Arizona, where my son attended the University of Arizona; California, where my brother lived; and yes, Las Vegas! Much to our surprise, we actually started to like it. In 1999, when I was offered a job as an assistant principal in a Hebrew day school, we decided to make the big move. At the time my husband was able to continue working in the collection field from our new home. Our family in New York was dwindling and moving away in small groups to Florida, Arizona, California, and here; there wasn't much binding us to New York anymore. Frankly, the traffic and snow shoveling were big detractors at that point in our lives.

Today it is twenty years since that move, and I can say it has been a good one for us. The weather, work opportunities, entertainment, friendships, outdoor sports, hiking, and fine dining all round out a good life. We both found work that was satisfying. I was an administrator in the public schools for seventeen years, fulfilling my desire to help students and mentor young teachers. Ron had a few jobs in the service industry: advanced planning, timeshare, placing temporary labor during the construction boom, and driving for a car service. Added to all this was the opening of the wonderful Smith Center, which brings Broadway shows and great performers here for us to enjoy. Our other love was the beach, which is only a four-hour drive away in Los Angeles. Visits to our children, grandkids, brothers, and sisters sweeten the drive!

One of the great opportunities our Las Vegas home provided us was hosting twenty middle schoolers from our daughter's private school in Nashville in September 2001.They were on their way to the national parks and planned on spending the night camping out in our backyard prior to their departure. We set up the backyard with sleeping bags and of course turned off the sprinklers. We barbecued franks and burgers and sang songs and had a fine time. The kids were surprisingly well behaved. They were polite and careful in the house.

All was going great until the next morning, which was September 11. After the deadly attack on our country, our house became a command post for these children, their teachers, and their parents back in Tennessee. Being in Las Vegas, a travel hub, they were able to hire a bus to take them home, but in the early hours of fear and confusion, parents frantically jammed the phone lines, making sure that their sons and daughters were safe. They were concerned about the next steps in getting them home. The journey to the parks was canceled, as the parks were closed and considered unsafe in case of further attacks. It was comforting to the parents to know their children were in the care of mature people, grandparents (that was us). We spoke reassuringly to them. That entire day was spent making travel arrangements for the schoolkids. We did the best we could entertaining and feeding them. Many were freaked out by the entire experience, as was the world. Being in a home as opposed to a hotel or a bus gave the kids some sense of grounding as one at a time they reached parents by phone.

There you have it—just one story of the many transplants who make Las Vegas their home, all the while *never* expecting to live here.

ALABAMA
ARKANSAS

Fun Facts about Arkansas and Alabama

- Sam Walton founded his Wal-Mart stores in Bentonville, Arkansas.—*50States.com*

- The fiddle was designated as the official state instrument in 1985.—*50States.com*

- Famous for its diamond trade, Arkansas is the only state where tourists can search for diamonds in their original volcanic source. At Arkansas's Crater of Diamonds State Park, visitors can dig through fields maintained by the park and are allowed to keep any diamonds they discover. The park also offers complimentary identification and registration of the gems. —*50 Astonishing Facts You Never Knew about the 50 States*

- Alabama was the home of George Washington Carver, who discovered more than 300 uses for peanuts.- *Fifty States and Fifty Fun Facts*

This is the story of **Max**, a fifty-seven-year resident of Las Vegas. He was born in Arkansas and had many jobs in his life, including farmer, naval officer, and newspaperman. Most of his life, he was a truck and bus driver, which afforded him the lifestyle of travel he enjoyed.

What he liked about driving was the freedom it gave him and the ability to see the wide-open spaces of this country. Family circumstances and job opportunities as a driver encouraged him to move to Las Vegas. The climate (not having to deal with bad winters), low taxes, and job security as a driver all made for a good living situation.

In his lifetime he lived in a number of states, including Alabama, Arkansas, Kansas, Missouri, Louisiana, California, and lastly Nevada. In 1982 he was driving for Trailways on a National Parks trip when he met his future wife, Mary Ann, a tour guide. She was a teacher in Massachusetts, and after they married, she taught in Las Vegas for nineteen years. They made a wonderful life for themselves here, building a home facing Lake Mead in Boulder City.

It was quite touching at Max's funeral in 2018 when Mary Ann recalled how humor played a wonderful part in their lives together, and they would laugh often about many things, especially his boyhood memories of being a farmer in Arkansas. Mary Ann expanded on this with three examples of Max's sense of humor, each from a different time in his life.

Max grew up in Arkansas, and as a third grader, he was not well behaved. In those years (the early 1940s) and in that state, corporal punishment was an accepted way of keeping students in line. His teacher hit him with a board for some incident. Two years later, Max was in fifth grade and had the misfortune of having for his teacher the husband of his third-grade teacher. When he again misbehaved, he received a nice whack on his backside. Max stood up, faced his teacher, and said, "Your wife hits harder than you do!" This no doubt emasculated his teacher and did not ingratiate Max to this man for the remainder of the school year.

On a trip to Salt Lake, Max and Mary Ann were riding an escalator behind a man wearing tight jeans. Mary Ann commented to Max, "He's got a cute bum. I'd give him a five." With a twinkle in his eye, Max ignored her reaction and said, "He's not a five. His name on the buckle is Frank."

Toward the end of his life, Max's hearing and cognition were not good, and he misheard many words. An example of this, combined with his sense of humor, was when Mary Ann asked him several times if he wanted to sit in his recliner. With her Boston accent, the word "recliner" came out more like "raclina," which he did not understand. She repeated this offer three times and asked if he heard her. Finally, he responded, "You want to ship me off to China?" Max maintained his sense of humor throughout his life during both good and bad times. It was his gift.

ALASKA

Fun Facts about Alaska

- Alaska has the longest coastline in the United States—6,640 miles. It is greater than that of all the other states combined. —*Fifty States and Fifty Fun Facts*

Dennis grew up and was educated in Brooklyn and Long Island, New York. At eighteen he trained for the US Air Force in Texas. He had a long and exciting career, retiring as a major in 2000.

Dennis was stationed at Nellis Air Force Base from 1985 to 1988. What he remembered about early Las Vegas was a remote but fun city, countrified with nickel slots. In 1997 his reason for moving here was the great climate. They had a family meeting three months prior to the move, at which time his family hated the idea, but they agreed to move to Las Vegas because that's what Dennis wanted. After they moved here, his son went to UNLV.

Dennis's time in Alaska was quite memorable and could not have been more different from his life now in Las Vegas. In 1983–84 he was stationed in the remote area in the Aleutian Islands called Cold Bay, close to Russia. He worked radar to spot and intercept unknown aircrafts that appeared on his screen, namely Russians. He lived there without his family, as it was too isolated.

He had some unique experiences when he returned to Elmendorf Air Force Base in Anchorage from 1988 to 1994 with his family:

He intercepted Russian aircrafts that were going to the United States, even though the Cold War had ended.

He became accustomed to seeing bald eagles, blue-green glaciers, the northern lights, Denali Park, wolves, Dall sheep, bears, lynx, caribou, moose, and puffins. He fished for trout, halibut, and salmon.

His son had a newspaper route, and there were mornings he could not deliver the papers because moose blocked his way!

Riding on the gondola to get up the mountain from one station to another, he experienced whiteouts where he could not see an inch in front of himself. Very scary!

After retiring from the air force in 1997 as a major, he started a second career with Clark County School District as a middle school teacher and coached Junior ROTC. Dennis was very surprised at how differently the school district was run compared to the air force. He expected more organization and order, and he was disappointed.

In his opinion, the best that Las Vegas offers is great weather, golf, hiking, and access to swimming at the beaches of Boulder City and California. One can reach all climates within four hours. He says that the worst thing about the city is that it has grown too big since his initial time in 1979, and there is too much traffic. While visiting the Neon and Mob Museums, he realizes how much Las Vegas changed in his four decades in Las Vegas.

Dennis experienced some interesting opportunities living in Las Vegas. When he was stationed at Nellis, he flew six F-16–connected emergency missions, following the coastline below the clouds.

As a part-time usher at MGM while he was teaching, he met some famous people, including Charles Barkley, Muhammad Ali, Paul McCartney (whose hand he shook), Simon and Garfunkel, Cher, and Madonna.

He commented, "To succeed in Vegas, you need to have a goal, a focus on something, whether it be a job or a passion for something." Dennis has had and still has this passion for his life, in his career in the air force, his travel experiences, teaching, ushering, and most recently just enjoying his life and his very connected family.

ALASKA

ARIZONA

Fun Facts about Arizona

- Arizona is a state full of natural wonders. It is a land of red rocks, canyons, monuments, mountains, and rivers. The saguaro cactus blossom is the official state flower. It is the largest American cactus, and it blooms during May and June.—*50 Astonishing Facts You Never Knew about the 50 States*

- The Castilian and Burgundian flags of Spain, the Mexican flag, the Confederate flag, and the flag of the United States have flown over the land area that became Arizona.—*50 Astonishing Facts You Never Knew about the 50 States*

This was a human interest story highlighting notable Las Vegans which was reported in the *Las Vegas Review Journal* on May 28, 2019 by Al Mancini, entitled "Henderson -based Group Assists Valley's Seniors" . The story intrigued me, so I included excerpts from it in my book.

Favil was a former military and commercial pilot who was the college roommate in Arizona of Ken Gragson in 1957. Ken, the son of

Oran Gragson, a past mayor of Las Vegas, brought Favil to Vegas to visit often during their college years. Afterward, Favil completed fighter pilot training and worked on a special project for an airline here in 1991, but he then returned to Arizona. He remembered how much he liked the excitement of the city and the many outdoor opportunities in Las Vegas, so when it was time to retire, he moved here.

In 2002, he and his partner, Chuck Davis, created an organization called Foundation Assisting Seniors (FAS). The organization's original purpose was to get medical equipment to those in need. In 2014, Favil learned that thirty-eight people had died at the Sun City Anthem retirement community, and their bodies went undiscovered for three to six weeks. He and Chuck found this news so shocking that they incorporated an additional new service that makes automated calls (in a program called "HowRU") to about a hundred seniors per day just to see how they are doing.

FAS started with assisting 360 people in 2002. Now they assist twenty thousand people a year. Equipment such as wheelchairs, scooters, crutches, and canes is kept on hand and distributed as needed, regardless of one's financial situation, and are lent out for as long as they are needed. Usually the loan is on a temporary basis until Medicare or other medical services engage. Favil says proudly, "We don't even look at finance. We don't care where you live or how much money you make. We don't care about any of that. You need it, you want it, you get it."

When asked about predictability for the need of equipment, Favil responded that it used to be predictable, but today it is uncertain how long a patient will stay in the hospital, whether he or she is transferred to a rehab facility, and what their needs will be when they return home. He states that sometimes their stock of thirty to forty wheelchairs is sufficient, but sometimes there is a wait, and FAS needs to purchase more chairs. These rentals are temporary, but patients are given an estimated time period of ninety days for use. If more time is needed, they can keep the equipment.

He told a story of an older lady whose husband had died, and she was left with a Lincoln car. She never learned to drive, so she was homebound. FAS delivered a scooter to her so that she could be mobile. She could "scoot" to the bus stop, go to the mall, and enjoy the day. This woman told Favil, "You are not Foundation Assisting Seniors, you're the foundation of angels." Their services are far and wide.

Favil would like to have more volunteers. He indicated that the current group of volunteers ranges in age from sixty to eighty-five, and sometimes the equipment is heavy for the older volunteers to lift and deliver. This seems like a wonderful and necessary service to people in need. Favil dedicated himself to the area of helping others, a continuation of the self-sacrifice he provided to his country earlier in his life. He stated, "The reward is seeing people who have a need, then filling that need, and to have them thank us."

Las Vegas is fortunate to have such a service-oriented son.

CALIFORNIA

California Suite

CALIFORNIA

Fun Facts about California

- The state motto is "Eureka," a Greek word meaning, "I have found it!" The motto was adopted in 1849 and alludes to the discovery of gold in the Sierra Nevada. —*50States.com*

Hope worked as a customer service supervisor for the Southern California Gas Company and lived in Southern California for forty-nine years. She and her husband moved to Las Vegas about eighteen years ago after vacationing here and loving the lifestyle, and because of the lower cost of living. They found great restaurants, music, plays, athletics, hiking, and sports, as well as the ability to ski close by. She commented that she was surprised at being able to ski in the desert. She loves the Summerlin community and the proximity to Red Rock.

Hope went on to buy and run a very successful Curves women's circuit-fitness franchise for almost fifteen years, incorporating her love of fitness and her excellent people skills. Hope spent time in the gym training women and helping them learn to use the weight-resistance machines on the circuit. She promoted a healthy lifestyle of good eating, exercise, and proper sleep habits, always with a smile and positive attitude and without judgment. She was a great role model to her clients, and I often joked with Hope that she was like the bartender in *Cheers*, listening to all the ladies' stories but without liquor! Instead she had her Starbucks and healthy breakfast in front of her each morning.

- The first person to receive a star on the Hollywood Walk of Fame was actress Joanne Woodward in 1960.—*50States.com*

Rosie was an elementary school teacher who called California her home for fifty-eight years. She and her husband planned on moving to Las Vegas upon retirement because they came here often on vacation. They loved the mountains and enjoyed the Las Vegas strip. They could live here in a home in Sun City for a fraction of the cost of a home in California. Their son moved here before Rosie and her husband to become a bartender on the strip, and then her daughter and her family moved here as well. Rosie lives in Sun City Summerlin and relishes the many opportunities for activities and friendship afforded her. She likes to quilt, sew, and volunteer to help others in her community who are not mobile. She often speaks about these pastimes with pride and a sense of accomplishment. She and her husband enjoy their happy "retired" life, but Rosie was surprised and disappointed in the traffic and increased number of accidents in Las Vegas thanks to the city's growth. This could be because people come from all over with different driving habits left over from their hometowns.

- Castorville is known as the artichoke capital of the world. In 1947 a young woman named Norma Jean was crowned Castorville's first Artichoke Queen. She went on to become Marilyn Monroe.—*50States.com*

After being raised and living in California for almost fifty years, **Joan** moved to Las Vegas because her then husband got a job as an architect at the MGM theme park in his chosen field.

Joan worked for many years on the newspaper *The Israelite*, selling advertisements. It was that job that helped her know everything that was happening in the community. This job gave her the opportunity to reach her potential in her career as far as going after what was meaningful, earning a good salary, and standing up for the underdog. She worked for a man who was both a great boss as well as a good friend.

She is amazed at the growth of Las Vegas over the past twenty years, and she has made a happy life for herself and her new husband. Joan said that she found excitement in this city thanks to shows and the strip. During our discussion, the topic of bonding with good friends became a recurring theme. She also spoke about all the good that she sees both in people and organizations in Las Vegas helping the underprivileged folks.

Joan recalled meeting some famous people through her work with Mike Tell, the owner of *The Israelite*. Mike was married to Patty Duke, and Joan met their son, Sean Aston, several times. At an event honoring Frank Sinatra after he died, she met Sophia Loren and members of the Rat Pack.

Today she is very involved in organizational work, fundraising for many causes. Both she and her husband, **Owen**, are extremely philanthropic, donating to many causes in Las Vegas and supporting the arts. She has met her calling presently working for Dress for Success, incorporating her knack for meeting people and her love of fashion. She stated that she helps people looking to make a new life by selling them gently used business fashions, which enables the clients to interview to secure work while feeling good about themselves. Joan feels very fortunate to have made wonderful friends as she's traveled the world and enjoyed her life in Las Vegas.

- One out of every eight US residents lives in California.
  —*50States.com*

The *Las Vegas Review Journal* carried a story written by Michael Scott Davidson, entitled, "Nevada's Speed of Growth Puts Silver State Natives in Vast Minority" on 1/25/19 about a young couple,

Alex and Emma who are examples of young people moving to Las Vegas.

After living all of his twenty years in Southern California, Alex came to Las Vegas to start his career teaching at Temple Sinai in Summerlin. He jokes that his apartment in Los Angeles was like a box, with no air conditioning, no pets allowed and no washer-dryer in his comple.

His fiancée, a personal trainer, "Emma was charmed by the Silver State's lower cost of living and the relief from the traffic and congestion of Los Angeles". (LVLJ, Davidson). She claimed, "It was like a small-town vibe in a big city." She felt that Vegas had all the stores and markets with which she'd grown up. Since living and working in Vegas, the couple purchased a three-bedroom home in Summerlin, an investment for which they would have had to wait years if they had stayed in LA. It has given them happiness and stability.

This story speaks to young people starting a life in Las Vegas, allowing them to be independent of their parents financially without sacrificing any of the creature comforts to which they have become accustomed. It is a very positive experience to begin a career without many of the financial concerns that others living in more expensive cities across the county have. Opportunity abounds for many young couples in Las Vegas, in addition to a healthy outdoor lifestyle for the athletically motivated among us.

Sheila lived in New York, New Jersey, and the Bay area of California before moving to Las Vegas almost twenty years ago with her husband, **Mark**. They had only spent one night in Las Vegas on their way to the national parks in Utah before moving here! She was a health-care executive for a well-known hospital in New Jersey. When the couple decided to move to Las Vegas, the good weather, favorable cost of living, absence of state tax, and good airport access all played a role in their decision. Sheila stated, "Because none of our family lives here, we couldn't move to a place without an airport close by."

Initially, Sheila was disappointed by the lack of an art museum and literary and art culture, even though she notes there is plenty to do in Las Vegas. Over the years, she has immersed herself in activities with UNLV, including the Black Mountain Institute and OLLI (Osher Lifelong Learning Institute). She has a subscription to the Nevada Ballet and regularly attends events at the Smith Center.

One of the impressive aspects of life in Las Vegas is the diversification and cultural exchange found as people create a second life for themselves in this city. It has been easy for Sheila to make new friends and expand her interests. Great weather, hiking opportunities, and proximity to nature are the best features of living in Las Vegas. However, having been a bicoastal person, she finds that not being close to the ocean is a drawback to living in Las Vegas, even though she gets a taste of water as she lives in a lovely neighborhood with artificial lakes surrounding the landscaping.

Sheila feels blessed by the wonderful friendships she has made and keeps busy with writing novels (three to date), attending book clubs, dining out, watching shows, and creating some artwork. She says, "Living in Las Vegas has given me time to create and enhance my originality of thoughts, energy, and drive, which I did not have until retirement." She has learned that it is helpful to have an open heart in her life in Las Vegas.

IN THE CAVE OF MEMORY

Sheila Paris Klein

SHEILA'S FIRST NOVEL

CONNECTICUT

Fun Facts about Connecticut

- The first automobile law was passed by the state in 1901. The speed limit was twelve miles per hour.—*50States.com*

- In colonial New Haven, pumpkins were used as guides for haircuts to ensure a round, uniform style. Because of this fashion, these New Englanders were nicknamed "pumpkin heads."—*50States.com*

For fifty years **Gina** lived in Connecticut. She was born, raised, and educated there. Her career was accounting.

She visited Las Vegas often on vacation and never wanted to leave, especially during the winter months. She found Connecticut winters brutal and welcomed the warmer climate of Las Vegas.

She had no family here until her daughter got a job and met her husband here after graduating from college in Vermont. At that point, even though Gina had always wanted to move to Arizona, she asked her husband to reconsider their plans. That was over twenty years ago. Gina stated, "Voila! We revised our plans and moved to Las Vegas instead of Arizona!"

Gina initially missed her lifelong friends back in Connecticut, and she says that it took a long time to find friends in Las Vegas.

As time went on, they found good relationships in this city, and she and her husband enjoy the benefit of living near their daughter.

It has been mentioned often that when older people move to a new city, they do not have the anchor of making friends through their children and their various activities. There needs to be different vehicle for coming together with new people, which isn't always easy to find. Living in a community like Sun City, Anthem, or anyplace with a clubhouse, golf course, or restaurants on the premises foster opportunities for meeting like-minded folks. Otherwise it is sometimes a difficult task.

COLORADO

Fun Facts about Colorado

- The world's first rodeo was held on July 4, 1869, in Deer Trail.—*50States.com*

- Colorado's southwest corner borders Arizona, New Mexico, and Utah. It is the only place in America where the corners of four states meet, and it is aptly called "the Four Corners."—*50States.com*

Sheila lived in Colorado for fifty years and worked as an executive assistant and paralegal. She vacationed here and found it unique, always providing her a good time. Her job as an executive for a hotel brought her to Las Vegas over twenty years ago, and it was a great decision at the time.

Even when she lost her job, she decided to stay in Vegas, because she was intrigued by the lifestyle available to older adults and the opportunities for an active, multifaceted life. Another thing that surprised her was that the summer heat didn't bother her, nor interfere with her schedule.

Nancy's story was similar to Sheila's in that she lived in Colorado for fifty years. She worked in compensation design and management, and payroll software design.

She vacationed here every two to three years, splitting the time between Las Vegas and California. Work eventually brought her here to live, but she and her partner maintained two businesses and a residence in Colorado. For them it has been a very good decision, even though at the time she didn't know that Las Vegas could provide such a "normal existence," complete with community experiences.

Nancy and her partner still go back and forth to Colorado, but when she is in Las Vegas, she says, "I love having a swimming pool here for my grandpuppies to swim and sunbathe." She is a dog person and enjoys the opportunity to walk her puppies in her community. She finds that walking her dogs is another opportunity to meet people with similar interests, while keeping up her walking routine.

PUPS ON A HAMMOCK

DELAWARE

Fun Facts about Delaware

- The Delaware Memorial Bridge is the largest twin suspension bridge in the world.—*Wikipedia*

Nancy, a teacher in Clark County School District, lived in Delaware for four years while attending college and moved on her own to Las Vegas in 1995. She had a friend who lived here and explained that Clark County was the ninth-ranking district in the country at that time. In the mid-1990s, it was very difficult to get teaching positions in her home state of New Jersey, so she decided to take a chance, figuring if she didn't like it, she would stay the year to finish out her contract and move back east.

Nancy came to Las Vegas in January of her senior year of college to interview and was hired in March to begin teaching that August. This was her first trip to Las Vegas, and her second trip was to look for an apartment after she secured a job as a teacher in CCSD. While all her friends were stressing out about job opportunities at the end of their senior year of college, Nancy was all set!

For her, the move to Las Vegas was a good decision. She married and has two accomplished children. However, as an educator, now a special education facilitator, Nancy is disappointed in the direction the school district has taken, with so much importance placed on standardized tests scores, as well as student assessments driving the direction of teaching. As a special education teacher and facilitator, she knows it is hard for challenged students to take these examinations and that it places great pressure on their teachers. I met Nancy many years ago when we both served on the board of Solomon Schechter Day School, and later she happened to be a teacher in one of the elementary schools where I served as the assistant principal. She was passionate about the special needs students she taught, always their advocate.

On a positive note, she is happily surprised about how the city has embraced the Vegas Golden Knights hockey team. The family are big fans and enjoy the opportunities presented to root for the "home team."

FLORIDA

Fun Facts about Florida

- Florida's Everglades National Park is the only place in the world where alligators and crocodiles coexist. You can tell the difference since the crocodile has lighter skin and a narrower snout, while the alligator sports dark skin and a broader snout—but you might not want to get close enough to determine these differences for either.
—*The Craziest Facts about Every US State*

Another teacher, another story. **Rhea** was raised and educated in New York. After marriage she lived in Florida for forty-one years, where she was a wife, mother, and third grade teacher. She vacationed many times in Las Vegas with her first husband, Marty, to visit their longtime friends Steve and Roberta. The four met on their honeymoon. They met in the elevator of the hotel they were staying at, having been married on the same day. That began a forty-year relationship culminating in a most surprising way!

Then a twist of fate: Rhea's husband died, and her best friend, Roberta, passed away. Rhea and Roberta's husband, Steve, got together, realizing their shared history was a comfort to them both. She moved to Las Vegas to be with him nine years ago, and they have created a full life: visiting his children in LA, then spending winters in Florida to visit her family. Rhea was surprised to see how many people are seeking friendships at any age, and she has been fulfilled by new friends made through Steve in Anthem. She expected more superficiality in people in Vegas, and she was concerned when she first moved here about the lack of roots that people have in Las Vegas because their histories are elsewhere. She figured that her past friendships were based on shared and common experiences: children, jobs, carpools, athletics. These potential new friendships in Las Vegas would have none of that backbone. So when Rhea was able to share in the friendships Steve and Roberta had cultivated, she was surprised at how easily she fit right in. They also traveled and made new acquaintances, as well as meeting people through activities at Anthem, where they live.

In her own words, her move to Las Vegas was made more by heart than by head. It was a bold move for Rhea, leaving a life of family, friends, and security. This was the beginning of a second life. Rhea told me, "Vegas is known to be a city of *chance*, and I took mine by moving to be with Steve." There is an old saying that "out of bad, something good will emerge." Both Steve's and Rhea's spouses lost their battles to cancer, his in 2003, hers in 2010, leaving devastated spouses.

When Steven called and said, "Do you think there is a chance for you and me to be a *we*?" Rhea was shocked! Now, nine years later, it turned out to be a wise and happy decision for both Rhea and Steve. When Rhea was asked how she knows they are living in the right city for them, she responded, "You wake up each morning with a smile, knowing you don't want to be anywhere else." She also said that she looks forward to returning home to Las Vegas after a vacation.

Asked whether or not living in Las Vegas has been helpful in taking care of herself, Rhea replied that even though her social circle is full, any time she spends alone allows her to be introspective and reflective, which at this stage of life is a very good thing! Sharing new experiences and developing patience has served her well in her move to Las Vegas.

GEORGIA

GEORGIA

Fun Facts about Georgia

- The carving of Confederate leaders on Georgia's Stone Mountain is the largest bas-relief carving on earth.—*Wikipedia*

Timing and life's circumstances often determine a move to Las Vegas. It was so for **Robin** about seven years ago. Her husband, **Sam**, left a family business of twenty-five years, and their daughter graduated from college, so it was a time for transition from one life to another. Robin had several careers in both Michigan (her first home) and Atlanta. She was a teacher, an author of several children's books, and mediated couples through divorce proceedings.

Climate was a factor for Robin—the desert climate helped her allergies, and she had vacationed in Las Vegas often to see shows and enjoy the entertainment. On the other hand, Sam had gone to college at UNLV, so he was familiar with the area and became the "team leader" when it came to house hunting. When he suggested moving to Las Vegas, Robin's initial reaction was the typical refrain of so many: disbelief! "Really, Sin City? Who really lives there?" Robin cried.

And so the search began. Their criterion was to find a place in the desert by the water—a tall order, but not impossible. Sam knew that there might be lakes to explore. As both are tennis players, proximity to courts was an important factor as well. Thanks to a knowledgeable and resourceful Realtor, they did lots of house hunting, yet nothing screamed, "This is it!" until the day before they were scheduled to leave. Sam found a townhouse on a small lake that they had driven by. However, it was gated, and they did not have access. The Realtor worked some magic and arranged a showing of the townhouse, with which they were immediately smitten. It was a home on Lake Sahara, and although it needed renovation, in Robin's words, it had "good bones." They felt there was solid potential in this structure.

They had work done on this house over the course of a year while still living in Atlanta. No easy feat. Once again, they trusted the Realtor, Carole, and her judgments and recommendations of contractors. Carole continued helping them acclimate by introducing them to friends and like-minded people in the community once they moved here. That is actually how we met them. We initially played tennis as couples, and then our friendship grew in other areas of interest, like movies, books, and boating. Whenever my grandchildren visit, we take kayaks out on Robin and Sam's lake, much to the enthusiasm of my grandkids.

Jump to the present. This couple enjoys the sunshine, dry air, and their boat rides on their "turquoise channel of water." Hiking, biking, tennis, entertainment, not having to endure heavy traffic, good food choices, and new friends have rounded out their happy lives here. Proximity to Mount Charleston's and Utah's skiing, the closeness of the airport for a quick getaway, and the California beaches fulfill the Vegas scene for them. To place the frosting on the cake, Robin studied and obtained her clinical license in social work and surprisingly started a career in counseling in her sixties! After having many careers, being able to help people toward mental health is Robin's true calling, and that has been realized by opportunities presented to her in what she termed Sin City—Las Vegas.

ILLINOIS

Fun Facts about Illinois

- The Chicago Public Library is the largest public library in the world, with over two million books.—*Wikipedia*

Louise's story is one that is different. How many people do you hear of who came to Las Vegas for good medical care?

Louise lived in Chicago for twenty-eight years, moved away for fifteen years, then returned to Chicago for four more years until relocating to Las Vegas in 2004. She worked in the field of advertising and marketing research and visited her father-in-law only a few times in Las Vegas. She thought the city was okay but had no desire to move here. As a matter of fact, she told her husband, Steve, she would move anywhere he needed to be *except* Las Vegas! Once again, the same refrain: "I never thought I'd live here!"

However, they moved for two reasons. After Louise was diagnosed with cancer, Steve's cousin (who is a doctor) would accompany her to medical appointments, and he would continue to do so in Las Vegas. Fate stepped in, and Steve took a job here as administrator of his cousin's radiology and surgery center, where Louise was guaranteed top and immediate care.

She had no expectations about the move to Las Vegas other than surviving cancer (which she has done). She and her husband in turn gave back to the city by opening a business that devoted itself to assisting people with physical needs. This came directly from Louise's ordeal with cancer and Steve's business experiences and acumen. Louise stated, "Since I have been able to live my life, I have felt it necessary to pay it forward, to do something that may have an impact on others. That's why our business of providing home care to those who need it appealed to me. That's why volunteering and working with the American Cancer Society and other cancer survivors gives me so much satisfaction."

When Louise was questioned about how her life changed by living in Las Vegas, she spoke about the obvious: her successful medical treatment. However, she responded positively to the diversity of the city, and she indicated that she has become more flexible, which encourages more people to enter her life. She believes that diversity has made her more open to different viewpoints and perspectives. She is more patient and forgiving, as well as less judgmental.

Louise and Steve enjoy the proximity to travel that Las Vegas living affords them, and naturally the variety of excellent entertainment, which they find so easy to enjoy.

"You become a survivor the day you are diagnosed," says Unell when she was interviewed by Diane Taylor on October 6, 2015 in an article entitled, "Louise Unell: Volunteerism a Result of Cancer." This was excerpted to supplement the oral and written information taken by Lynn Rosenberg about her work volunteering for American Cancer Society and Susan B. Komen Fight Against Breast Cancer. Loiuse is a believer in research dollars because she participated in a clinical trial of a new breast cancer treatment which saved her life. She, like so many other survivors chose to be a "warrior". We wish her continued good health!

IOWA

IOWA

Fun Facts about Iowa

- Iowa is known as the Land of Covered Bridges.
  —*Lynn Rosenberg*

- The world's largest painted ball resides in Alexandria. The four-thousand-pound baseball with a fourteen-foot circumference is the creation of Michael Carmichael, who began the project more than fifty years ago after dropping a ball in paint; he now adds another coat or two every year.
  —*50 Astonishing Facts You Never Knew about the 50 States*

- Corn, corn, and more corn! The United States is the leading producer of corn in the world, followed by China.
  —*Fun Facts about Iowa*

The Volcker recession hit Iowa hard in 1981–82; it was said to have been the worst downturn in the economy since the Great Depression. Few jobs were to be found in Iowa at this time. Teachers were being laid off, and **Glenda** loved her job as a special education teacher. At the time, Las Vegas was booming and hiring. The thought was Las Vegas was "recession proof." Both Glenda and her husband moved here for employment.

The couple had no friends or relatives here, but jobs were here, so her husband moved in 1981, rented a place to live, and "checked it out" while Glenda stayed in Iowa with their four-month-old baby. She did not resign her job in Iowa until she was sure they could make a life in Las Vegas. Glenda said, "We left a utopian community for an unreal world." The family planned to be here for a year or two until the economy in Iowa improved. That was over thirty years ago!

In review, Glenda rated their move both good and bad in all areas:

- School districts. They are rated poorly, but she found good schools for herself to work in and for her children to attend.

- Weather. They had to look for areas to picnic and entertain, but when they'd listen to weather reports throughout the country, they soon realized Las Vegas has the best of all places.

- People. They're the best and worst. They had to learn not to trust everyone, since they'd moved to a melting pot, unlike the homogeneity of Iowa. However, they were able to find sincere and caring friends who'd also emigrated to Vegas. Most everyone would say to them, "You think you are here for a short time, but you'll stay."

The couple are bicyclists and can ride in Las Vegas all year long. They travel in the early morning in the summer and late in the day in the winter. They vacation now back in Iowa and look forward to riding in the RAGBRAI, a bicycle ride across Iowa, as well as spending quality time with friends and family.

It surprised them that they could ski here, which they learned to do at Mount Charleston. They started to tell their friends from home that you could ski on snow on Saturday in the mountains, and water ski on Sunday at the lake. Glenda commented, "Where else can you do that in the same weekend?"

Another activity that transferred for them was the rodeo scene. They used to attend many small rodeos in Iowa. Now they go to the National Finals Rodeo in Las Vegas, as well as other smaller rodeos.

So in conclusion to a very interesting transplant story, this couple still misses Iowa and their friends, but they feel like, in Glenda's words, "they have grown a new tree" here, having raised children who had great teachers in the public schools and went on to receive scholarships to attend the colleges from which they graduated. The unreal became real!

LOUISIANA

Fun Facts about Louisiana

- Louisiana's Lake Pontchartrain Causeway in Metairie is the longest over-the-water bridge in the world, at twenty-four miles.—*Wikipedia*

"Old is gold," says **Judith**. "Older is a much better word than old."

Judith has had a very successful life through a modeling career, coordinating fashion, and creating camouflage cosmetics. She lived and worked in several states before settling in Las Vegas twenty-five years ago. In the 1970s she lived with her first husband in New Orleans, a city with a history of three-hundred-year-old bars, contrasted to the ever-changing face of Las Vegas. It was in New Orleans that she opened a cosmetic boutique of her own called Let's Face It. She still has ties to New Orleans, because two of her four grandchildren reside there.

Let's Face It had an exclusive line of cosmetics and perfumes and became an instant success. Lines of people squeezed into the small store each Saturday. It was the place to be to get ready for the proms, parties, and balls for which New Orleans is noted. It was awarded the "The Mecca of Makeups and Makeovers."

In the 1980s Judith moved to California to become the training director and community outreach person for the Aida Grey

Company, lecturing about how to look younger. At that time, she worked with plastic surgeons to help patients use concealers after surgery for burns or scarring. She then came across a cosmetic pencil made in Germany and developed her own pencil formula. When doctors asked her what it did, she replied, "Simply everything," and thus the name and pencil were born! In 1986, this pencil was featured as the editor's choice in *Allure* magazine.

Judith moved to Las Vegas from California to be with her future husband, George, who had a health-care business here. She did not have a good feeling about possibly living in Las Vegas, but commuting to see each other became difficult. Then in 1994 the Northridge earthquake destroyed her home. This was the same year that the Judith August Cosmetics Solution was formed.

During her modeling career, Judith came to Las Vegas for work on location and did not like the atmosphere. She was hit upon, and she felt there was no culture; it was a "seedy" place. Also, her memory of Las Vegas was affected by her father, who was a gambler. She said, "I can't live here...It's barren."

After her initial negative feelings about moving to Las Vegas, her expectations were varied. She loved the mountain views, made good friends, enjoyed good food, grew her company, and felt more comfortable with each passing year. She still has a life in Los Angeles, but it diminishes as time passes. Judith still misses the ocean and her children.

Today she works in partnership with top cosmetic laboratories in the United States, and together they create relevant products that cover and conceal just about everything for everybody. In 2012, she wrote *Gotcha Covered*, a compact guide to camouflage makeup. This guide is a culmination of a forty-year career of tips and lessons, which she passes on to her readers. Judith says, "Looking good is not superficial. It measures health and image and encourages self-esteem."

This story was written after many oral histories taken between Lynn Rosenberg and Judith, and with permission to use excerpts by Joan Peck, in an article she wrote entitled: "Judith August and the Magic of Serendipity" for the Spring/Summer issue 2019 *Chic Compass Magazine* .

JUDITH AS A YOUNG MODEL, AND JUDITH TODAY

MARYLAND

Fun Facts about Maryland

- Havre de Grace, Maryland, boasts the world's largest decoy museum, with over 1,200 innovative floating sculptures.—*Wikipedia*

This lady is a geologist who grew up and lived in Maryland until college and then moved to Las Vegas over forty years ago, because her then husband, who was a physician, was offered a great opportunity. She had never visited nor vacationed here, and she was scared at first about the Sin City reputation. However, it turned out to be a great decision due to the availability of outdoor activities, good private schools, low cost of living, and easy access to world via air travel.

She found many opportunities to study and create jewelry living in Las Vegas, with its proximity to Tucson's yearly Gem and Mineral Show each February. She has lovely rock sculptures displayed in her home. She has been able to pursue her craft by living and working in Las Vegas. The proximity within minutes to Red Rock Canyon and hours to Zion and Bryce enabled her to further learn about the rocks she studied in college.

She was surprised to find out that unless you work in the gaming or hospitality fields, you really don't have to have anything to do with the hotels. People who don't live here are under the misconception that that going to hotels and gambling are all that residents do.

Living in a 24-7 town is something that she takes for granted until she travels outside Las Vegas and is unable to find food varieties as well as constant entertainment and abundant natural beauty.

MASSACHUSETTS

Fun Facts about Massachusetts

- The first World Series was in 1903 between the Boston Americans (which became the Boston Red Sox in 1908) versus the Pittsburgh Pirates.—*Fifty States and Fifty Fun Facts*

After over forty years living in Massachusetts, **Mary Ann**, who was a teacher, moved to Las Vegas over thirty years ago. Her story is quite different from others in that her prior experiences in Las Vegas had to do with one-night "stay overs" while leading tours through the national parks during the 1980s. On many of those trips, her future husband, **Max** (see the Arkansas entry), was a driver for Crimson Travel. Through these tours, the couple had many opportunities to talk and share life's experiences with each other.

In 1986 she was touring with a group in Colorado, and Max was on a trip in Wyoming. He surprised her by calling her and proposing marriage! As Mary Ann quipped, "We never really had a date, but on some trip, the altitude must have hit us." She accepted his proposal immediately! She always said that Max made her laugh all the time. What a perfect ingredient for happiness!

They were married at the Little Chapel of the West and started their lives together in Las Vegas. The city provided good job security for Max, who continued to drive tour buses. The favorable climate and low taxes created a "trifecta" in the couple's decision about where to live. They built a home in Boulder City, and Mary Ann resumed her career teaching elementary school. I met her during the years I was the assistant principal at Treem Elementary. She was a natural as a teacher and integrated her travel experiences into the curriculum to make social studies more interesting for her third grade students.

For Mary Ann and Max, it was a great decision to move here. She made wonderful friends through teaching, and the weather was a real plus compared to the New England winters! The only difficulty has been living so far away from her family, preventing her from seeing them on a regular basis. But Mary Ann has always been a traveler and is not shy about getting on a plane anytime for any reason. She has seen the world, yet her real love is Disneyland.

MICHIGAN AND PENNSYLVANIA

Fun Facts about Michigan

- The cereal bowl of America, Battle Creek, Michigan, produces the most cereal in the United States.—*Fifty States and Fifty Fun Facts*

Fun Facts about Pennsylvania

- Lancaster, Pennsylvania, is home to a large population of Amish people. —*Lynn Rosenberg*

Kathe was born, raised, and attended college in a small town in Michigan. During her first marriage, she lived in Lancaster, Pennsylvania, where she taught, raised her two sons, and was active in community and synagogue work. It was there that she opened and ran a Montessori school before changing her life and moving to Las Vegas in 1996.

Denny was born in Philadelphia but grew up in Lancaster, where he married and raised his three children. He ran a family camera shop and then worked selling Prudential insurance. "I came to Las

Vegas in 1980 on vacation with my first wife and was dazzled by the sights and the sounds of the city," says Denny.

Kathe had never been to Las Vegas, but she had a cousin who moved here to attend the Le Cordon Bleu College of Culinary Arts. That was her only connection to Las Vegas. After their respective divorces, Kathe and Denny connected. Kathe knew Denny through the Jewish community and synagogue in Lancaster. They both had children the same age and knew the same people. Both Kathe and Denny wanted to leave their hometown, and they discussed places to live. Phoenix came up, but Denny found work in Las Vegas selling Xstampers to businesses, libraries, and post offices. So Kathe came to Las Vegas to be with Denny and see how Las Vegas suited her. Kathe came without any game plan. She was running away from her old life, looking to begin a new one. She had no commitment nor job, and she stored all her furniture for the time in case it didn't work out. Kathe states, "Not only did I gamble on living in a new city, not knowing anyone, but I gambled on a relationship."

Eventually, her life took shape, and she found a job teaching in a Jewish day school. She continued to teach in several Jewish day schools and eventually opened and ran the library at the Solomon Schechter Day School for many years until 2018. Denny worked for several insurance companies, selling annuities and financial products to the employees of Clark County School District. In 2010, Denny retired, and now, he says, "golf is his job."

In 2008 Kathe and Denny were married, and they continue to live and enjoy life in Las Vegas. It gave them what they needed. Denny enjoys golf and occasional gambling, and the weather is a plus. Kathe says that the quality of life, their home, pool, friends, and good restaurants make for a good life. They have several children and grandchildren between them and are able to spend time visiting and traveling back east, as they are now both retired.

When questioned about the worst thing about living in Las Vegas, Kathe referenced her terrible sense of direction. She doesn't like traffic and has a difficult time finding destinations. Well, this writer can certainly attest to that! When we became friends, we were invited over to their house. This was before Google Maps, so we relied on Kathe's directions. Aside from the terrible rainstorm that night, we drove around in circles based on her poor directions. What should have been a twenty-minute trip took us about ninety!

Asked about what she has learned living here, Kathe responded, "To be yourself, be the person you always were." Kathe made friends who, she found to be "kindred souls," even though she thought she'd left all those people behind in Lancaster. In her opinion, it is healthier for the couple to live here because of the good weather and the ease of living. They swim in their pool every day during the summer, and Denny is an avid golfer all year round.

Kathe and Denny have spotted many famous people in their twenty-three years living in Las Vegas. They often run into Marty Allen at the bank, Ben Vereen at Wow buying records, and Carlos Santana at the bar at Mastrioni's, and they sighted Nicholas Cage at the same restaurant (we were with them for that star sighting). At a golf tournament, Kathe spoke to Shirley Jones and told her that she loved her performance in *Oklahoma!* Shelley Berkeley actually visited Kathe's fifth grade classroom and spent time with her students, talking about their goals and aspirations.

Kathe says that she made the right decision to come here. It has not been a disappointment, even though it has not been all smooth sailing. Initially, she did not like living in a town founded on gambling, with a glitzy strip and void of culture, but she admits culture has been slowly coming. The transient nature of people also was an issue. But they made a huge leap and took a gamble moving here, and it has been the best thing for their relationship. It was love that brought them to Las Vegas, and love is why they stay.

MINNESOTA

Fun Facts about Minnesota

- Minnesota boasts the Mall of America, the largest single-building mall in the country, which also includes the largest indoor amusement park in the world.—*Wikipedia*

Lydia lived in Clearwater, Minnesota, for twenty-three years and owned her own party-planning business. She worked as an event coordinator for local community events and planned children's birthday parties.

In 2011, her boyfriend asked her to move across the country to Newport Beach, California, for a company merger. They packed their belongings and made the big drive, only to find out the deal had fallen through! However, they decided to stay in California, and her fiancé built his own company from the bottom up. That was the good news. But his accountant told him he should move to Nevada to save money on taxes. So after eight months, they packed up again and moved to Las Vegas, got engaged, and bought a home.

Lydia's initial thoughts about moving to Vegas were negative. She said, "I had never ever been to Vegas before I moved here. I never planned to live here, and I actually never planned to even vacation here." She imagined Vegas to be chaotic, crowded, and unsafe. To her great surprise, since moving here in 2011, she has fallen in love with the Spring Valley community. She cannot imagine ever moving back to her home state of Minnesota.

MISSISSIPPI

Fun Facts about Mississippi

- Coca-Cola was first bottled in Vicksburg in1894.
  —*Fifty States and Fifty Fun Facts*

- The *Mississippi* River is the largest in the United States and is the nation's chief waterway. Its nickname is Old Man River.—*Most Important Facts about Mississippi*

Jackie is a senior employee assistance specialist with the Clark County Fire Department. She has lived in Las Vegas for four years. Her home state was Mississippi, where she grew up, joined the US Marine Corps, and was trained as a mental health counselor with a specialty in addiction therapy.

About fifteen years ago, Jackie, her husband, and two children vacationed in Las Vegas, and they did not like anything about it, especially the strip and the absence of family life. She told her husband, "Moving to Las Vegas is out of the question and not even open for discussion." They returned to Mississippi, but after many years back there, they decided they hated the humidity and it was too traditional. They were ready for a change.

Four years ago, the time was right, and their children were old enough to fend for themselves. They moved to Las Vegas, and

Jackie followed her calling to work in the field of mental health. Her husband retired and plays golf, and her children work in the city. Her daughter is a downtown project greeter in Container Park, and her son is a cook and aspires to be a chef.

When the family first moved here, Jackie was a substitute teacher, but she kept applying to work for the county in the field of mental health because of her training. At that time there were no jobs in mental health working with the fire department due to budget cuts. As the city and the fire department expanded, and as the need for counseling grew after the Route 91 Harvest Festival shootings, additional counseling was greatly needed. The governor reinstated those jobs.

Getting to know people so that Las Vegas feels like home is something that surprised Jackie. She became more outgoing by meeting people through work, entertainment, and restaurants. She feels like she is contributing to her adopted city by helping people work through mental health and traumatic issues. When asked about a lesson she has learned living in Las Vegas, she responded, "Underestimate no one."

Jackie thinks that the best part of Las Vegas is that people are less judgmental than in Mississippi. When asked about the worst issue, she said homelessness. She is making a contribution by helping people through trauma and tough times and perhaps preventing them from ending up living on the street.

NEBRASKA

CARHENGE

Fun Facts about Nebraska

- Carhenge is a replica of England's Stonehenge. It's located near the city of Alliance, Nebraska, in the High Plains region of the United States. Instead of being built with large standing stones, as is the case with the original Stonehenge, Carhenge is formed from vintage American automobiles, all covered with gray spray paint. Built by Jim Reinders, it was dedicated at the June 1987 summer solstice. In 2006, a visitor center was constructed to serve the site.—*Wikipedia*

Steve and Judy lived in Omaha, Nebraska, for over forty-five years before relocating to Las Vegas over twenty years ago. Steve and his family owned a wholesale produce business, and then for several years he owned a Dollar Rent a Car franchise. Judy's parents owned a luggage store, where she worked to help them out. She was a stay-at-home mom until she went back to college at thirty-nine to get a secondary teaching degree, and she taught in Omaha for two years before moving to Las Vegas.

They came to Las Vegas twice on vacation: once in 1974 and then again in 1984. They thought it was a fascinating city, but Judy said to Steve, "It's fun to visit, but why would anybody want to live here?" Yet they moved here, as many do, for jobs. Steve had an opportunity to work for a food wholesaler here when his family sold the business in Nebraska. In addition, Clark County School District was hiring massive numbers of teachers, many from out of state. The economy played a significant role also. The ability to buy a home at a reasonable price, low property taxes, and no state tax incentivized them as well. As most have said before them, it was hard to leave family behind, but they viewed it as an adventure. They were typical Midwesterners, never having lived anyplace else.

They love the winters in Las Vegas, compared to the brutal winters in Omaha, but they were surprised by the consistency and intensity of the summer heat. Also, they were surprised by the number of people here who thought that Nebraska was not sophisticated nor a good place to raise children. They found it difficult making new friends and were disappointed in the lack of friendly services, pride, and work ethic here. In her words, "It took transitioning my brain from Midwestern thinking to Las Vegas thinking by learning to go with the flow. It was quite an adjustment."

Big turning points in enjoying Las Vegas were their home in a neighborhood they loved, a teaching position Judy enjoyed for many years, membership in a health club, and finding pets to love. They made meaningful relationships with other couples, and the weather in spring, fall, and winter was captivating, a nice change from the harsh Nebraska winters.

Steve loves to meet and talk to people. He is usually up to speed on all the news in Omaha, and he keeps up with many of his old friends as well as family in Nebraska. They have made us aware of all the good people and traditions coming out of Omaha, like Johnny Carson and Warren Buffet, just to name two famous people. However, Steve has been fortunate in meeting well-known people in Las Vegas. He regaled me with stories of people he's spoken to in Las Vegas whom he never would have met in Omaha! Here are a few tales:

- Steve met Tony Curtis while selling cars. He greeted Tony with, "Hello, Bernie Schwartz!" Tony was so surprised that he responded, "Nobody has called me that in years!"

- Steve sold a car to Dean Martin's daughter. She said, "You might know of my father, Dean Martin."

- He saw David Brenner walking in town, Jon Voight at an IHOP, Matt LeBlanc at the Rio, and Rod Stewart at In-N-Out Burger.

- While walking his dog in Desert Shores, he ran into Mike Tyson, who was jogging with a friend. Mike stopped and asked if he could pet his dog, and he commented that Kobe was a beautiful animal.

Steve is clearly a "magnet to the stars!"

NEVADA

Fun Facts about Nevada

- Las Vegas, Nevada, has the largest number of hotel rooms of any city in the world, with over sixty-two thousand on the strip alone.—*Wikipedia*

Susan has had a love/hate relationship with Las Vegas for over sixty years. She moved here with her family when she was five years old because her father wanted to be a "big fish in a little pond." Her parents were from the East Coast, New York and New Jersey; then they moved to California, and finally in 1953 they moved to Las Vegas. Her father opened the first credit department store in Las Vegas across from the main post office, which now is the Mob Museum!

Susan was starting first grade when they moved here, and she recalls moving from a green place to a brown place. She remembers that it was too hot to play outdoors, and what was outdoors but a desert anyway? It was a cross between a cowboy and Mormon town. She actually refused to sing "Home Means Nevada" when it was taught to her in school!

Back in that day, Las Vegas was considered a really small town, with only sixty thousand residents. The only three hotels Susan remembers were the Sahara, Flamingo, and the Sands. Kids were allowed to swim in the hotel pools, and she even took lessons from a lifeguard named Gordon Scott. He was "discovered" and ended up replacing Johnny Weissmuller as Tarzan! Her senior year she worked at the Sahara in the cash cage, and she found the jingling of the slots exciting. She went through the public schools and excelled socially. Susan witnessed the transition from Mob to corporate ownership of the hotels.

When Susan went out of town to college, she realized that growing up in Las Vegas was not like growing up anyplace else. She compared notes with her roommates, and it was determined that all the "big shot" parents of her classmates from other cities were doctors, lawyers, and politicians. In Las Vegas, a big shot was a gangster! She had a different vocabulary than the rest. In her own words, "I sounded like a Damon Runyon character!"

After college, anxious to escape Las Vegas, Susan took jobs in several major cities—Rome, Washington, DC, and Mexico City—and had to remind herself that everything that looked old was "quaint," as opposed to Las Vegas, where everything was new. Her job was to audit tax returns of Americans working abroad. She had six-month assignments in consulates and embassies for the international operations of the IRS. She found being away from Las Vegas very exciting. However, coming home for the first time made the words "purple mountain majesties" make sense.

After all the traveling she has done in her life, Susan learned that living within your own home with your own family and friends is what makes a home. Susie is comfortable with the growing sophistication she has seen evolve in Las Vegas.

NEW HAMPSHIRE

Fun Facts about New Hampshire

- Artificial rain was first used in Concord in 1947 to fight forest fires.—*Fifty States and Fifty Fun Facts*

Our next story comes from an anonymous administrator with Clark County School District. She lived in a small town in New Hampshire for the first twenty-five years of her life. She only had a second cousin who lived in Las Vegas during the time she lived in New Hampshire.

Her story gets interesting when she visited this cousin in Las Vegas in 2006 and met a man she knew from her past who intrigued her. She got married spontaneously! After they were married, the couple decided to look for a place with a warm climate and opportunities in education for herself. Her thoughts were Florida, Nevada, and California. She ruled out Florida because of the hurricanes. California was eliminated because she had lived there already, so they ended up in Nevada. This turned out to be a fantastic decision for her, because she had the opportunity to go back to college and continue her career in education and administration. She and her husband purchased a home and raised three children in a warm climate in a small community within Las Vegas.

She never thought that she would raise her children in Las Vegas. As a child growing up in a small town in New Hampshire, she never worried about gun violence in schools, nor was she concerned about riding her bicycle around town or walking by herself or with a small group of friends. As a parent, she is deeply concerned about the safety of kids in school and the overall crime within the Las Vegas community.

The great weather has been a happy surprise. She prefers Nevada's dry heat and hot weather to the humidity and cold winters of New Hampshire. The smaller community in which she lives provides opportunities for extracurricular activities and enrichment, which was more than she expected. There are wonderful organizations that offer opportunities to enrich communities, which translates to activities and programs for our youth. She says, "I have met many amazing, kind, and generous folks in my thirteen years living here."

It seems apparent to this writer that people interviewed for my book who are in the field of education seem to find rich opportunities for their own children because it is important to them. Others who complain bitterly about the school system tend not to seek out positive educational experiences and programs for their own children. Perhaps Clark County School District needs to improve their outreach and publicity to the public about the fulfilling courses, clubs, sports, and musical programs available for enrichment.

NEW JERSEY

Fun Facts about New Jersey

- New Jersey's Atlantic City has the world's longest boardwalk, measuring 5.5 miles.—*Wikipedia*

Marsha was raised in New Jersey and lived there for thirty-five years. She relocated to New York State for twenty years before moving to Las Vegas around eighteen years ago. She was a speech pathologist back east, which she continues to be here. My husband, Ron, and I met Marsha and **Steve** in a parking garage many years ago when Ron and Steve realized they recognized each other from working with a mutual colleague on Long Island. We went out to dinner only to discover many connections Marsha and I had through our work in education on Long Island as well. I have found connections such as these to be quite common when meeting new people in Las Vegas.

Marsha had no family who lived here, but she became interested in Las Vegas when her best friend moved here. Also, her then boyfriend, Steve, had business in Las Vegas, and she would join him and "vacation" for weekends, as well as continuing to visit her friend who had moved here. They were smitten with the city—good restaurants and shows, and no cost for parking other than a tip (at least not back in 2015, when this was written). "Can't get better than that," joked Marsha.

After visiting Las Vegas, Marsha and Steve felt they would take a chance, and it turned out to be a good decision. She is still able to work and play, and they have made some wonderful friends along the way.

She is surprised that she is still working as a speech pathologist, having expected to only work for a year or so. Their lives are filled with travel, community activities, synagogue volunteering, and good friends. Steve does important work with the Jewish War Veterans, advocating for improvements in the quality of their lives, and has found a receptive environment in Las Vegas. Steve hopes to fulfill his promise to the veterans, fighting for better housing, drug rehabilitation, and plentiful and nutritious food. He served as post commander for many years.

In listening to oral histories, it amazes this author how many people used the phrase "take a chance" about their move to Las Vegas. Is that a coincidence that this is a gambling city, or is it just a popular turn of phrase? I wonder if people's descriptions about moving to other new cities comes with the same phrase. Perhaps a question to explore!

NEW MEXICO

Fun Facts about New Mexico

- Taos Pueblo has been inhabited for over a thousand years.—*Fun Facts about New Mexico*

- New Mexico has more PhDs per capita than any other state.—*Fun Facts about New Mexico*

Nicole was raised in Missouri but attended four years of college in Las Cruces, New Mexico. She has been a resident of Las Vegas for almost twenty years, and prior to that she vacationed in Las Vegas every year around Easter with her extended family since 1985. She spoke of vivid memories of those trips. She enjoyed the Ethel M Cactus Gardens, the Hoover Dam, and the good weather. She recalled that the streets around the airport were dark, and Pecos was a dirt road. Half of the streets present now weren't there at all in 1985. She talked about how clearly she could see the sky and stars on those trips.

Niki met her husband-to-be, **James**, in college at New Mexico State University, where she studied education and he studied physical therapy. After graduating college, James didn't have a future as an athletic trainer if he stayed in New Mexico, so the couple came to Las Vegas in 2000, thinking there would be more opportunity to practice physical therapy in Las Vegas. They soon discovered that PT was not licensed here at that time, and it was a more conservative and litigious field to enter than in New Mexico. In addition, the small market was saturated. While James thought about staying in Vegas and joining the air force, Niki hated living here, missing the intimacy of the Las Cruces community.

As many have done before and will do after, James found a "break-in" casino in the Barbary Coast, and he started his training as a dealer. The term "break-in" referred to a kind of internship for a person who desired to have a career as a dealer. He then went to Excalibur and currently works as a table game supervisor at the New York–New York casino.

Niki found her niche as a classroom teacher (at Treem Elementary School, where I supervised her), then special education teacher, and now a school librarian. All the while she learned to be patient, open minded, and an advocate for culturally diverse students. As a librarian, she says, she can incorporate all that was good about being a classroom and special education teacher. Niki is surprised that she now believes not everybody needs to go to college to succeed as she used to think. So many jobs and occupations are needed in the city that require training and technical skills but not necessarily a four-year college diploma.

When asked what she found surprising about living in Las Vegas, she said something very profound. Up until the Route 91 Harvest Festival mass shooting, at which fifty-eight people died and over five hundred were wounded on October 1, 2017, she never considered Las Vegas to be her home. However, after the outpouring of help through donations, blood drives, and many stories demonstrating how people went above and beyond expectations for the victims and families, Niki felt grounded. She felt appreciative of the community's support.

When asked about what she saw as a disappointment living here, she said sadly that the school district and class sizes are too big. This makes for a difficult situation regarding school discipline. Often teachers' hands are tied as far as what they can do with a student who misbehaves.

Niki touts many wonderful things about living in Las Vegas. She loves Spring Mountain Ranch, the Clark County Wetlands Park, and the Smith Center. All of these, as well as her library job, are great reasons to enjoy life in the city. She says that as big as Las Vegas is, she believes it is small in the "six degrees of separation" vein regarding connections to people, places, and events. She believes that to succeed, an individual needs patience, open-mindedness to diversity, and a good sense of direction. She laughed about how the roads are forever under construction and changing.

ROUTE 66 PASSES THROUGH 8 STATES:
CALIFORNIA, ARIZONA, NEW MEXICO, TEXAS,
OKLAHOMA, KANSAS, MISSOURI AND ILLINOIS

NEW YORK

Fun Facts about New York – *State Facts, New York State.com*

- New York borders six other states as well as Canada.

- New York City was actually the capital of the United States when George Washington took his oath of office at Federal Hall in 1789.

- New York is the third-most populous state in the United States, behind only California and Texas.

- The state flower is the rose.

- The most popular nickname for this state is the Empire State. "I Love New York" is the state song.

- The NYC subway system, which opened to the public in 1904, is one of the largest public transportation systems in the world.

- New York was the first state to require people to use license plates on vehicles.

- NYC is the birthplace to the United States' first pizzeria, which opened its doors in 1905.

- Ellis Island in New York Harbor was an entry point for millions of immigrants hoping to become American citizens between 1892 and 1954.

THE BIG APPLE
A NEW YORK FRAME OF MIND

Sara is a hairdresser in Las Vegas who was born in Puerto Rico and lived there until she was five years old. Her family moved piecemeal to New York in groups of three siblings at a time. She worked, lived, and raised sons in New York for over fifty years until moving to Las Vegas fifteen years ago.

She and her husband, **Miguel**, moved here to be with their sons and to avoid dividing them up. They vacationed in Las Vegas after one son moved here, and they made a down payment on a house on the second day of their visit! Sara made the decision to move because her son wanted to watch his brothers grow up. However, she left a loving family behind in New York. The excitement of Las Vegas was great, even though it took her a long time to adjust to living here. "People seemed to care more about gambling than being friendly or saying hello," says Sara. This became boring and old fast. Sara is disappointed in the "walls" that separate people who might be great neighbors living next door to you. She recalls that it was not like that in New York.

As years went on, her sons married, and she has five wonderful daughters-in-law and eight grandchildren who are close and constantly visiting with her, stopping by for a meal, and dropping off kids for babysitting. She has her steady customers in the salon and paints in her spare time with great talent. Sara contributed four sketches for this book: Alaska, Georgia, Iowa and New York. In her own words, she's "making the best of it." She still misses New York with its energy and constant motion.

Barbara was a fifty-six-year resident of New York, where she was a teacher and grade advisor in the New York City public school system prior to retiring to Phoenix.

She and her husband, **Barry**, ended up in Phoenix because Barry's uncle was the first medical doctor once Arizona became a state. Barry had been coming to Las Vegas since he was a boy and knew he wanted to retire to the southwestern part of the country when the time came. However, after living in Phoenix, they found restaurants closed very early, which was an inconvenience, and they were bored with the lack of entertainment.

They had a bad feeling about relocating to Las Vegas because on an earlier visit, Barry was hit by a car and injured, but they "took a chance" and have never regretted the move. They love their lives in Sun City and have never looked back. "Las Vegas is a twenty-four-hour town," says Barbara. "We love Sun City, which has an enormous number of clubs, so we never get bored."

Lynette and her husband lived for almost sixty years in upstate New York. She worked in banking. They vacationed here and decided to retire to a major city with much more to offer than their simple rural hometown. Living in upstate New York had its definite identity: the beauty of the greenery, simplicity of life, changes in seasons, and very cold winters lasting from October until May. Having attended college in upstate New York, this writer can vouch for the unrelenting cold!

The great weather and favorable cost of living played a major role in their selection of Las Vegas as a home. The couple was pleasantly surprised at the ease with which they were able to become involved in activities and develop a social life. They have been living here over a year and were concerned that after having the same friends for almost sixty years, they would not be able to connect with new people. Through volunteering and participating in various clubs and organizations, Lynette reports that they have made wonderful friends, love their home, and have plenty of old friends visiting them. Lynette says, "I just must remember that I am not on vacation, even though I live in a vacation destination. It has increased my waistline and decreased my sleep!"

We find that many people move to Las Vegas after retirement and need to adapt to a different way of making friends. Early in life friends are made through one's children and their school and various activities. Parents carpool, go to meetings, discuss social and school events, and often depend upon each other for help in those early years with children. During the working years, connections are made through daily interactions with coworkers. However, as senior citizens, people have to find friends in a different manner, and often there is the desire but limited opportunity if they are shy. But if they avail themselves of clubs, entertainment, volunteerism, and religious institutions, they can be very successful and fulfilled, as my stories reveal.

Many Mondays, I meet local icons Shecky Greene, Pat Cooper, Pete Barbutti, Dennis Blair, and others for breakfast. Yep, we laugh a lot!—*Ed F. in Diane Taylor's article for the Living Las Vegas website, August 11, 2019*

Ed used to sing when he served in the Air Force National Guard. It was there that he met Mel, who was a comedian who later went on to perform on the *Arthur Godfrey and His Friends* show in the 1950s. Ed and Mel lost touch then but reconnected many years later. Mel told Ed that he and his brother had opened a dry cleaning business in Las Vegas (which later became Al Philips). Mel invited Ed and his wife, Julia, to visit, and Mel spent a week showing them the sights. He took all this time because he really thought Las Vegas was special and wanted to encourage Ed and his wife to move here by showing them the best of the city. Ed and Julia had been to Vegas in 1950 and 1958 (when there wasn't much to see) and then again in 1988. This time, in 1991, it was a different city! Ed asked his wife what she thought about relocating from Long Island to Las Vegas, and before the sentence was out of his mouth, Julia said yes. The fact that she loved to gamble and that they both had had enough of New York winters facilitated their decision.

When Ed lived in New York, he introduced desktop computers and word processors to the Hewlett Public School District, where he worked for twenty-six years. After he retired, he said, "It took four people to replace me!"

A sculptor and teacher of art and photography, Ed spends much of his time photographing and enjoying talented singers and performers in Las Vegas. "This feeds my love of music and my craft of photography at the same time," says Ed. He also spends time back in New York visiting his son David and his three grandsons, who all have inherited his creativity in one form or another.

He is now ninety years old and has had a very interesting life meeting and photographing celebrities and politicians around Las Vegas: Robert Goulet, Joe Williams, Shecky Greene, Clint Holmes, Bob Anderson, Anthony Hopkins, Bill Clinton, and Barack Obama, just to name a few. In addition, since he moved here, he has done photography for Realtors and staging companies, which helped him initially learn all about the Las Vegas Valley, which he truly loves. These are opportunities that, by his own admission, he would not have had if he stayed in New York. His art and creativity have grown and developed during the twenty-five years Ed has lived here. In addition, this photographer is an accepted member of the entertainment community through his amazing photography. Seen at many openings, events, concerts, and shows, Ed carries his camera all over, because he never knows when that perfect picture will appear for him.

This story was written by Lynn Rosenberg with permission for the use of excerpts from an article written by Diane Taylor on August 11, 2019, entitled: "Photographer Ed Foster Tells The Stories" and Neal Portnoy's whimsical sketch of Ed Foster in the article.

SKETCH OF ED FOSTER BY NEAL PORTNOY

NORTH DAKOTA

Fun Facts about North Dakota

- North Dakota's Jamestown hosts the world's largest buffalo statue at over twenty-six feet tall and forty-six feet long.—*Wikipedia*

For about five years, **Joe** and **Etta** performed in Las Vegas nursing homes and retirement communities. She played the accordion, and Joe danced. She took up the accordion because Lawrence Welk, who grew up in a rural town not far from Etta, made the accordion popular in North Dakota when Etta was growing up in the 1930s and '40s. Las Vegas was a place she couldn't even imagine as a child!

Etta was born in a rural town in North Dakota in 1928, and it was her whole universe. She never heard of many things because as a child she worked in the field of her family's farm and went to church. That was her life.

"Today Etta is a vivacious ninety-one year old lady who moved to Las Vegas via California in 1979 after visiting the city often with a friend in 1975". (LVRJ, Przybys). She discovered that she loved everything about it. She was exposed to the most excitement in the world. She says that there isn't a new casino that opens that she doesn't experience, nor an old one that implodes over which she doesn't cry! Etta smiled and said, "After seeing Dean Martin, Frank Sinatra, and Dinah Shore perform, I thought I'd died and gone to heaven."

The *Las Vegas Review Journal* carried this story on 8/11/19, "The Tune of a Life Well Spent," written by John Przybys helping to promote Etta's book called *No Bull*, which she wrote to teach her children and grandchildren about her early life in a small rural town the likes of which they cannot conceive.

OHIO

Fun Facts about Ohio

- The first electric traffic lights were invented and installed in Cleveland in 1914.—*Fifty States and Fifty Fun Facts*

Sandy lived in Ohio her whole life except for four years from 1995 to 1999, when she moved to Las Vegas. Her family lived in a small conservative farming town in Ohio where the population was mostly white Protestant or Catholic. They did not even know any African Americans or Jews until they moved to Las Vegas. She was a teacher in Ohio and lived near a large, very closely knit family.

Prior to moving to Las Vegas, Sandy and her husband, **Vernon**, made about twenty trips vacationing here and loved every minute. They decided to move to Las Vegas. Their one daughter and four grandchildren relocated with them. What they loved about the years they lived here was the diversity. Sandy said that it was awesome to work with all people and stated, "People are people everywhere." Working for four years in a Jewish day school atmosphere, she had many different experiences from her years teaching in rural Ohio! It was obvious to this writer, working in school with her as her supervisor, that Sandy had a real respect and appreciation for a culture and religion that was quite different from her upbringing in Ohio. She took pride in learning about Judaism—its holidays, traditions, music, and artifacts. She actually learned alongside her students and relished in the exposure she was experiencing on a daily basis, knowing she would never have had such diversity in Ohio.

The family moved back to Ohio because they missed the rest of their family, who remained in Ohio. Fast-forward to the present. With four children and twenty-one grandchildren, they still come back yearly to vacation here, because Las Vegas is a magical place for them, affording them entertainment, natural beauty, buffets, and gambling unparalleled anyplace else. It was on most recent visit that, coincidentally, they rented a house across the street from us in Desert Shores, and we reconnected over drinks and laughed about past school experiences.

OHIO

We don't mind when people ask, "Do you really
live in Las Vegas? Do you live on the strip? In a
casino?"—*Joe Boyd*

Joe is the founder and president of Rebel Pilgrim, a full-service
creative agency with offices in Las Vegas and Cincinnati. His story
is a little different than most, although like Sandy and Vernon, Joe
did move back to Ohio after living in Las Vegas for ten years. He
joked, "We don't mind when people ask, 'Do you really live in Las
Vegas? Do you live on the strip? In a casino?'" Las Vegas was a place
that worked for him.

This article ran on: rebelstoryteller.com/lasvegas on August
26,2014 entitled: "11 Reasons Why I miss Living in Las Vegas"
which I referenced. Even though he moved back to Ohio, he still
considers Vegas home for the following reasons:

1. The sunshine—294 days a year

2. The quick escapes—Red Rock, Zion, Lake Mead, Mount
   Charleston…

3. The food—great restaurants and fun local spots

4. The hours—almost nothing closes in Las Vegas. (Coming from New York, this writer doesn't agree.)

5. The casinos—there is nothing like this in the Midwest.

6. Nevada Day—a holiday off (every state should have one of these)

7. Downtown—Zappos and Container Park

8. Emerging improv/comedy scene

9. Sunday morning spirituality, whether a desert walk in the sunshine or church service

10. The people, composed of many transplants—runaways, cowboys, dreamers, partiers, casino dwellers, and entertainers

11. No state income tax

So there you have it: the many reasons that have been stated previously validating the things that people love about Las Vegas.

OREGON

Fun Facts about Oregon

- Oregon's International Museum of Carousel Art in Hood River claimed to have the largest collection of carousel horses in the world.—*Wikipedia*

Sue's home state was Montana, but she and her husband relocated from Hood River, Oregon, almost thirty years ago when Sprint acquired Centel in 1993. Once the integration was complete, they resisted the powerful magnetic pull of the Sprint corporate flagpole in Kansas City and kept their feet planted firmly in Las Vegas among the mountains of the west. They had no family here, nor had they ever vacationed here.

Sue and her husband, **Kip**, felt "disappointed in how quickly anything nice gets dumbed down in the ongoing cycle of robbing Peter to pay Paul." The unprecedented rise and fall of Las Vegas has been an education for them, and Sue said, "Living in Las Vegas has been like living the *Reader's Digest* version of *Ancient Rome: The Rise and Fall of an Empire.*"

The writer of this book opines that not everybody is won over by the weather, easy lifestyle, and plethora of activities in Las Vegas! This couple obviously was a not a fan of living in our city. I met them while working on a landscape committee in Desert

Shores, where we all live. They were filled with many good ideas during our meetings. They would provide spreadsheets of facts and information to recommend what types of plants the development needed. So in a sense, they turned their dissatisfaction into positive work, which they contributed to the community.

PENNSYLVANIA

MAYOR CAROLYN GOODMAN CASINO CHIP

Fun Facts about Pennsylvania

- Philadelphia is famous as being the birthplace of the United States of America, since both the Declaration of Independence and the Constitution were written here.
  —*Interesting Facts about Pennsylvania*

Carolyn has served the people of Las Vegas by volunteerism and leadership in many nonprofit boards, charities, and service organizations.—*Excerpted from the official Las Vegas website, "Biography of Carolyn G. Goodman," www.lasvegasnevada.gov*

Carolyn Goodman was elected mayor of Las Vegas for the first time, winning 60 percent of the vote, on July 11, 2011. She succeeded her husband of fifty-five years, Oscar, who was mayor for his term limit of twelve years. It is the only known instance of a spouse succeeding a spouse as mayor in the United States.

Goodman is now in her third and final term. The Goodmans have served Las Vegas for a total of over twenty years!

Mayor Goodman is a driving force in the continuing development of the city of Las Vegas, enabling it to take its place among the major cities in our country. Whether she's championing non-profit social services, tourism, a football stadium, educational improvements, industry, or development of the medical community, Carolyn is a great resource.

An earlier major accomplishment was Mayor Carolyn Goodman's founding of the prestigious Meadows School in 1984. She oversaw the day-to-day running of the school—its budget, staffing, building, and curriculum—for twenty-six years. Never in that time did Goodman ever take a salary for herself. Even though she retired from that job in 2010, the school continues to thrive and produce generations of high achievers who are admitted to fine colleges and universities.

What brought the Goodmans to Las Vegas? The couple moved from Philadelphia in 1964 with only eighty-seven dollars between them! Oscar was recruited to work for the district attorney's office, and Carolyn worked as a vocational counselor for the department of labor, training and building employment opportunities for African Americans when the city of Las Vegas was segregated. Even then, Carolyn advocated for opportunities for the underprivileged. She then worked in the hotel industry, in addition to raising four small children while Oscar was a "Mob lawyer" traveling the country.

Mayor Carolyn Goodman continues to work with pride to develop our city, making tremendous contributions to its future. The couple's life in Las Vegas is a tribute to service, and this writer is sure that their success is something they may not have anticipated when they moved here in 1964!

Parts of this story were excerpted from the biography of Mayor Carolyn Goodman website, www.las vegas nevada.gov.

RHODE ISLAND

Fun Facts about Rhode Island

- Rhode Island was the last of the original thirteen colonies to become a state. Its distance from north to south is forty-eight miles and from east to west is thirty-seven miles.—*Fun Facts about Rhode Island*

Kim, a teacher's assistant for special education in Clark County School District, moved to Las Vegas from Providence, Rhode Island, almost thirty years ago.

She and her husband raced greyhounds at Lincoln Greyhound Park in Rhode Island and won the world's richest greyhound race two years in a row, 1987 and 1988, earning over $100,00 each year! After they retired from racing greyhounds, her husband came to Las Vegas to work with Kim's father, removing asbestos from mills and schools. Then on a vacation they decided they wanted to live here.

The couple followed her family's move to Las Vegas, and for a time they all lived together in one house. That was very challenging—different habits, food allergies, different bedtimes, neat versus sloppy living, and the like. Kim reported that to be somewhat hard to handle, even though there was a lot of love involved. The contrast between life in a small town in Rhode Island and Las

Vegas in 1993 was amazing! Kim stated that Sundays were family days in her hometown: church, park or beach activities, supermarkets and liquor stores weren't open, and life was quite simple. Kim joked, "In Rhode Island, if your drive to work is more than fifteen minutes, you work too far. It is small, quiet, and cozy."

The state was predominately Catholic, with each ethnic group living in their own sector of the state. Italians, Portuguese, Blacks, Hispanics, French, and Irish all stayed segregated in that manner. She said that there could not be a greater contrast living in Rhode Island to her life in Las Vegas in so many ways. The diversity of people all living together was so different from Rhode Island. This has made her much more aware of different cultures, races, and religions and has facilitated more open-mindedness for Kim.

When they moved to Las Vegas, Kim was shocked at the size and population of the city, which is larger than the entire state of Rhode Island! Crime and violence here was another surprise. "We never even heard of carjackings until we moved here!"

It took time to acclimate to life in Las Vegas, but after so many years, Kim and her family love their home, family, and life in Las Vegas and are very happy and fulfilled living here.

NEW YORK

SAUDI ARABIA

GREECE

GERMANY

SOUTH CAROLINA

IRELAND

EGYPT

RHODE ISLAND

LAS VEGAS

Fun Facts about South Carolina

- The first tea farm in the United States was created in 1890 near Summerville.-*Fifty States and Fifty Fun Facts*

This is a story of diversity. **Kellie** lived in an amazing number of places before settling in Las Vegas twenty-two years ago.

She was born in Lockport, New York, which is near Buffalo. During her childhood and teen years, her family moved around often due her stepfather's job in the Federation of Communication Services (FCS). As a young teen, Kellie lived in Saudi Arabia but could not attend school past the age of fifteen there, so she attended boarding school in Athens, Greece, and moved again to Bonn, Germany, where she graduated from high school. Another stop in Egypt and then a semester in Ireland rounded out Kellie's international visa by the time she was twenty-five.

After returning to Buffalo and attending a community college there, she decided to finish college in another location. She picked the College of Charleston in South Carolina because she wanted to get away from snow, and this college's tuition was a reasonable cost to the family. Having lived in so many places and experiencing all different cultures and people, Kellie relished being with a diversity of people. However, what she found in Charleston was a kind of reverse discrimination toward white people. She found a divide in the early 1990s between black and white students, which was very disappointing to her.

After college, Kellie spent time with a family in Ireland, then spent three months in Rhode Island until her uncle became ill and Kellie returned to Buffalo to be a support to her mother. After her uncle died, Kellie was at a crossroads in her life about where to settle. Her mother and her stepdad were moving to Tennessee, and it was at this point that Kellie decided she needed to be on her own. Fate stepped in, and Kellie found herself interviewing with a representative from Clark County School District. She accepted a teaching job in August of 1998, a job that continued for twenty-two years. Kellie had never been to Las Vegas, but as many have stated before, she took a chance.

Kellie liked living in Las Vegas immediately upon her move. She met another teacher with whom she had student taught, and this young woman helped Kellie get an apartment and start her new life. She expected to stay two years, yet it turned into twenty-two years, which surprised her greatly. She made some wonderful friends and shared years of closeness with her students and their parents. She was only missing what most people express—family.

She has enjoyed her years in Las Vegas and indicated that her favorite outing is hiking at Red Rock, especially when visitors come to town. She recounted a fun time when she was coming out of a casino and walked right into Woody Harrelson. He was very courteous and agreed to a picture.

When Kellie was asked how living in our city changed her, she replied, "When I was young, I accepted everything. Then I learned to question and act in a manner that was true to my feelings." She learned to stand up for herself, and people she met along the way helped her to find her voice. This has actually led to her recent decision to return to New York, as she has become disenchanted with the school district in Las Vegas. As a kindergarten teacher, she feels that class size, paperwork, and constant testing accountability have all changed what she loved about teaching.

We wish Kellie well in her move and have no doubt that with all her experiences living in many places, she will find her niche—maybe writing about her interesting life!

TENNESSEE

Fun Facts about Tennessee

- Nashville's Grand Ole Opry has been broadcasting on the radio since 1952, the world's longest continuous radio show.—*Wikipedia*

Ray and **Bev** have lived in Las Vegas for forty-two years. They each hail from small towns outside of Memphis, communities in which they grew up, attended college, and taught elementary school. The couple decided it was time for them to leave Tennessee, specifically because Ray wanted to be a high school teacher and athletic coach, which was not available to him in Deyersberg, Tennessee, at that time. Ray joined the US Air Force and was stationed at Nellis Air Force Base, which he says was a good decision at the time. That brought them to Las Vegas to live. After about three years, Ray knew he would have been moved to another city if he stayed in the air force, and by that time he had come to love Las Vegas's weather and wanted to stay.

Ray started volunteering to coach sports. As time progressed, Ray climbed up the sports ladder and combined coaching with teaching in Clark County School District. He was open to new opportunities, taking those that were offered to him, specifically becoming a member of the state athletic board. He said that he was at the right place at the right time and that he was not afraid to get involved. One promotion led to another until he was made head of athletics for the school district, a position he held for many years until his recent retirement.

Bev taught outside Memphis and then for many years in Las Vegas. She finally became the principal of Booker Elementary School for over ten years. The ultimate recognition came when a new elementary school in the Southwest Valley was named for her in 2017. She said that there were "unlimited educational opportunities in Las Vegas." The value the couple placed on education was transferred to their two daughters, who attended colleges in Nevada. One of their daughters has an administrative position with Clark County School District, and the other is a director of admissions in an elementary district in Texas.

Now, "educational opportunities" is not a typical phrase one hears living in Las Vegas. However, I believe it is true that if students and their parents want a good education, they need to avail themselves of the clubs, educational opportunities, and musical and athletic programs that are offered. Too often, parents complain about the school system, yet they do not eagerly reach for chances presented to them to enhance their experiences. I saw this many times during my seventeen years working in the school district.

Bev is still involved in consultation work for the school district and continues to be active in her church activities. Ray is happy playing golf most days and relaxing during retirement. Las Vegas has been good for the couple and facilitated many circumstances for success for them within Clark County School District to serve students and the communities surrounding various schools.

Ray said that he was surprised at the continuous growth of Las Vegas that he has seen in the four decades living here, and that growth brought unlimited opportunities to this couple. Interestingly, when asked about his take on what is needed to succeed in Las Vegas, Ray responded, "Moderation, discipline, and balance." He was of course referring to the many temptations in this city—gambling, buffets, night life, and sun exposure, just to name a few. Ray said that he never thinks about moving back to Tennessee after over forty years living here. "You could never start over where you came from in such a changed world."

VERMONT

MAINE

MISSOURI

MICHIGAN

OKLAHOMA

OREGON

MASSACHUSETTS

LAS VEGAS

Fun Facts about Vermont

- Vermont is the home to the Vermont Teddy Bear company, the world's largest online bear company, with more than five hundred thousand annual sales.—*Wikipedia*

Fun Facts about Maine

- Maine's West Quoddy Head is the most easterly point in the United States.—*Wikipedia*

Jane and **Tom** have lived in many places, even though they were born on the East Coast, Jane in Hinesburg, Vermont, and Tom in Massachusetts, where they grew up, meeting in Vermont during college at the University of Vermont. Jane spent summers in Maine studying zoology. She had a position in upper management for a hospital when they lived in Massachusetts. Tom is a doctor who trained in Missouri, practiced in several communities in Massachusetts, and opened a rural hospital there. They have always been a couple who loved nature, the outdoors, traveling, and most recently bird watching. They assumed they would stay in Massachusetts after retirement, but fate had other plans for Jane and Tom.

One of their daughters moved to Las Vegas after marriage to be near her in-laws and found a job as a teacher. When that marriage didn't work out, Tom and Jane decided to move to Las Vegas five years ago to help with their two grandsons, even though having visited Las Vegas often for medical conventions in the 1990s, they could not imagine raising children nor grandchildren here. Jane was candid about her feelings, stating, "I am a religious person. We almost never go to the strip, and I was concerned about the images of naked women, showgirls on billboards, and the influence of gambling for my grandsons. However, I found a church that I fell in love with, which was a surprise. We found golf and the great outdoors, and we have been happy, and especially it has been a good decision to help our daughter raise her children."

Jane found Las Vegas to be a hub to connect to nice people, and she does not miss the snow of the East Coast. Even though the couple enjoys the outdoor activities in Las Vegas, their last home was set on ten acres in the country, so their backyard here seems to be an adjustment. They have beautified their surroundings with birdhouses, plants, and flowers, which make them comfortable, but Jane still feels that there is little privacy compared to the previous home. They still have a huge recreational vehicle, which they use to travel all over the country, especially making trips to see their other three children, who live in other states.

Jane lives by the credo that "home is where the heart is" and that they can be happy anywhere. The biggest surprise about living in Las Vegas is how much outdoor activity there is to enjoy, and to succeed, Jane stated that one needs independence to explore and find pleasure. Water aerobics and going to a gym have helped to maintain her good health. In addition to spending time with her grandsons, enjoying the outdoors, traveling in the RV, and reading, Jane finds time to volunteer to help older adults. She boasted that they have been to every state in the United States except Hawaii! I'm glad there is still someplace to explore for this couple who seems to have done it all.

VIRGINIA

Fun Facts about Virginia

- Virginia is the home to the Pentagon, the largest office building in the world, containing over sixty-eight thousand miles of phone lines.—*Wikipedia*

Susie Johnson, an author and teacher's assistant in special education, lived in California and Iowa but most recently in Virginia before relocating to Las Vegas almost twenty years ago.

Her parents had retired to Las Vegas, and Susie joined them afterward. She visited often but never dreamed of living in Sin City. However, she reached a point in her life, as revealed in her memoir, where she needed a fresh start. She says that it was an amazing decision from which wonderful things have emerged for her: many friends, a husband, a career in education, and a memoir of her life with bipolar disorder, which has helped many people.

Las Vegas has definitely grown on her, and she was "surprised by the beauty of Red Rock, never expecting to find such a great place to hike." In the past few years, since publishing her book *Some Dreams Are Worth Keeping*, she has achieved both recognition and confidence in her own life. She knows that she has been fortunate living in Las Vegas, which offered her a receptive and supportive environment to write her book and to speak publicly about mental illness. Susie has brought this much-needed topic into the light and has opened many conversations and provided assistance to those struggling as she previously was.

SUSIE'S MEMOIR

WASHINGTON

Fun Facts about Washington

- Boeing, in Seattle, makes aircraft and spacecraft such as the Lunar Rover. This was the vehicle used by astronauts on the moon.—*Fifty States and Fifty Fun Facts*

This is a most unique story about **Jessica** starting in Australia, traveling to Washington State, and ending up in Las Vegas. It's built around atomic testing, blackjack strategies, gambling, legal research, and celebrities.

Jessica was born in Australia after WWII. Her mother was an Aussie war bride. She was a foreign-born American baby boomer. Jessica was brought as an infant to the United States, where the family eventually lived in Richland, Washington, outside the atomic reservation at Hanford.

The huge nuclear reservation isolated them. They were the same twenty thousand people for twenty years living in a government-built All American City, not knowing that they were the unofficial sister city of Ozersk, Russia, their rumored ideal government-built town. Despite the canning of uranium, Jessica and her parents had a near-idyllic existence on the surface. The common people didn't know they had to care about the physics of uranium. It was such an unusual population that several studies have been done about them.

She went to high school with a boy who was born in Las Vegas. Presumably his father had something to do with the atomic testing in Las Vegas, and he was moved to the atomic reservation outside Richland. Jessica and her family didn't understand why. Everyone's job was classified. No one could talk shop after work.

After high school Jessica got married and lived in several places around the United States. After she and her husband divorced, she attended college in her thirties, majoring in mathematics. Because the employment market was poor when she finished college, she did something very unusual. A retired mathematics professor proposed they become partners, doing something that was relatively new and just being successfully refined: card counting blackjack players. They formed the MIT Blackjack Team. They were so successful that for a significant period of time, Jessica was achieving win rates two standard deviations above the norm! "When you are successful at blackjack, you don't become famous," she quipped. She developed parameters to play, and she didn't want to play for visibly outrageous sums and attract the worst maneuvers of the casinos. They were in the process of switching from beating people up in the back room to charging them with trespassing. "They absolutely don't let you play if you know how to play a winnable game," she said. During this time she flew in and out of Vegas every month and got to know the city as well as a resident or a dedicated tourist.

After several years Jessica changed careers and began doing legal research. She was not surprised to learn how many early blackjack card counters have a similar occupational profile.

In 2002 the economy was suffering, even with post-9/11 grants. The only city in the entire country that had a positive employment situation was Vegas. Because of these factors, she moved to

"Los Angeles East"—Las Vegas—along with a surge of people who had lost their jobs on the East Coast following the bombing on September 11.

It actually took her a while to find a permanent job, but Jessica said that the lure of Las Vegas was strong, especially the lower cost of living compared to the surrounding West Coast states. The quality of life is high, with several thrift stores, no state income tax, and local newspapers full of casino buffet coupons. Half the population takes advantage of offers meant for tourists, and the other half hasn't seen the strip in decades! Slowly you get used to active twenty-four-hour days, and it is much easier to take care of life's business when stores have extended hours. Soon she realized it would be a strain to live otherwise. Also, Las Vegas has the best weather in the United States—maybe a tiny earthquake every twenty years to remain colorful. Now that the city has completed its flood control project, it has no natural disasters.

"Meet-ups" were invented in New York City after 9/11. People here can easily adopt a cynical attitude, but Jessica was impressed when she first started coming here how many people—almost everyone—did something every year for a charity. Meet-ups also really took off here: running, cycling, movie-going groups, professional writers, photographers, and actors were prevalent. She stated that it is still one of the few places in the country where a single woman can go out alone whenever she feels like it, because she is in a casino with hundreds of others and no one knows she is alone. We forget about this simple freedom.

Of course, over the years, she said, she's played with lots of celebrities and the movers and shakers that control from the back of the house. "That's where you find out the truth." But most interesting to her was the resort workers' response: "Your privacy is safe as long as you behave and tip well, or act like you love the staff. But if you behave badly and don't tip, somebody in the press is going to get the story."

Jessica related a fun story about celebrities. Long ago she was playing blackjack at the relatively new Mirage. A nice kid sat down. He had a couple of girls behind him he was ignoring, and a wildly dressed friend that would buzz the table occasionally. She said that she used to get privately angry when an under-twenty-one-year-old kid would sit down and play, but she never said anything because she had to act like she was on vacation and didn't care. But this kid seemed to catch on real fast that Jessica knew what she was doing. When she moved to another table, he followed her. She knew that had to stop, or she would have to leave. Knowing the floor, she told him she didn't like to play with underage kids. This should have alarmed him, but it didn't. He told her they weren't under twenty-one; they were the famed rock band Guns N' Roses! That was the first and last time she complained about underage players. You never know for sure someone else's story.

Jessica's story is probably the most authentic Las Vegas story in this collection, and learning about our city from the inside track was fascinating and quite illuminating. The rest of us are so conventional!

WEST VIRGINIA

Fun Facts about West Virginia

- West Virginia's New River Gorge bridge is the world's third-largest arch bridge at over 1,700 feet long.—*Wikipedia*

Terry moved to Las Vegas over twenty-five years ago from West Virginia. Her husband attended flight school in California as a young man, regretted moving back east after his training, and wanted to retire to the west when the time was right. Then their neighbors in West Virginia moved here. It was at this point that Terry and her husband, after vacationing here several times, decided they had an appetite for Las Vegas. Terry actually worked here for two summers as an assessor for the National Board for Professional Teaching Standards and lived with her former neighbors during those summers.

Contrary to what she thought about the move, it was *not* a good decision that first year. It was hard on her daughter and her, the transition being much more difficult than expected, as they lacked close friends and relationships in Las Vegas. They missed what they had taken for granted in West Virginia.

However, time has improved her feeling about the city because of the excellent weather, great entertainment, and food, as well as having a successful career as an elementary teacher. Becoming a grandmother has been very fulfilling, and being close to her family will probably be the reason the couple will stay here after retirement.

WISCONSIN

Fun Facts about Wisconsin

- The typewriter was invented in Milwaukee in 1867.
  —*Fifty States, Fifty Fun Facts*

- The Green Bay Packers are the only publicly owned NFL team that is also a nonprofit.—*David Schwartz*

Taylor's family followed her to Las Vegas from Wisconsin twelve years ago. She grew up in Wisconsin riding horses and working odd jobs as a student. She wanted to leave Wisconsin and lived with her aunt in California for a few months until her family moved to Henderson. The family rented a place there until their home was built, which gave them a chance to become familiar with the area.

Taylor indicated that when she left Wisconsin, it was the right time, because she had no real ties there educationally or romantically. At nineteen years old, it was time to start something new.

Her family discussed the move, and she preceded everyone else. Her dad had a career as a linebacker for the Green Bay Packers, which took a major toll on his body. The constant changes in weather, pressure, and bitter winters in Wisconsin made it very hard for him to function normally. "My family ended up in Las Vegas due to my dad's inability to live normally in Wisconsin due to major injuries he sustained playing football. He needed warmer weather to function normally," explained Taylor. The fact that her parents had business contacts in Las Vegas, coupled with the favorable weather for her dad, made Las Vegas a great spot for relocation. Both parents grew up in Southern California before their years in Wisconsin. This move brought them closer to extended family.

The move was a great one for Taylor as well. It led her to continue her education, start on a career path as a teacher in Clark County School District, and meet her husband. She says that she will never lose her Midwestern values, but she loves the restaurants, entertainment, and hustle of Las Vegas. She enjoys all the beautiful communities Las Vegas has to offer.

She was surprised and disappointed at the same time about how much she loved Las Vegas! Part of her wanted to have reason to move back to Wisconsin, where her lifelong friends lived, but Las Vegas really felt like home. Another surprise was meeting another Midwesterner here, whom she married. "The city feels like a big city but a very small world at the same time," explained Taylor.

WYOMING

Fun Facts about Wyoming

- Wyoming's Yellowstone National Park is the world's first national park, spanning nearly 3,500 square acres.—*Wikipedia*

Sherry lived in Wyoming for nineteen years and has been in Nevada for twenty-two years. Most of her family lives in Arizona, and only her husband's uncle lived in Las Vegas. She has been teaching in Clark County since 1999.

Her husband, **Scott**, worked in the coal mines in Wyoming until there was a threat of job layoffs. During that time Sherry worked toward a degree in elementary education. The couple moved from Wyoming to Winnemucca, Nevada, where her husband got a job working in the gold mines. Since Clark County School District was desperate for teachers in 1999, she applied and got hired, which brought the couple to Las Vegas. Even though they wanted to get closer to Sherry's family in Arizona, Las Vegas was a more favorable destination. It had outdoor walking trails, entertainment, and food availability twenty-four hours a day. The added bonus of being a state without state income tax incentivized the couple as well. At that time, their daughter was a senior in high school, and Sherry and Scott wanted her to finish her education in Winnemucca rather than Las Vegas, so they waited to move.

The negative aspect of Las Vegas for the couple was that they did not want to raise their daughter here. However, Las Vegas has proven to be good for the couple. Sherry has a good job as a special education teacher, and Scott works for Caterpillar. She states that she would not mind staying after retirement, but they have forty acres in Arizona to which they will probably return after her parents pass away. The weather in both Las Vegas and Arizona is comparable, and that is a plus. She feels that Vegas has a lot to offer, so long as she stays "off the strip!"

THEY ALL CAME TO TEACH

Georgia

Hawaii

Idaho

Indiana

Kansas

Kentucky

Michigan

Missouri

Minnesota

Montana

Oklahoma

South Carolina

Texas

Utah

GEORGIA

Fun Facts about Georgia

- The Girl Scouts were founded in Savannah by Juliette Gordon Low in 1912.—*Fifty States and Fifty Fun Facts*

Ashley moved from Savannah, Georgia, after living there for all of her thirty-two years, and she found her initial experience in Las Vegas to be disappointing. She was a graduate student in Georgia and worked in the home daycare field. Her husband was offered a great job in one of the hotels, which they felt couldn't be passed up, and she sought work in Clark County School District as a school counselor.

After being uprooted from their families, they put a bid on a house only to be disappointed in the upgrades that were promised but not delivered. Fortunately, they were able to back out from this deal. That was her first taste of Las Vegas. They also became aware of how little they felt they got for their money compared to Savannah home prices. But they found a home they felt was comfortable, safe, and surprisingly family friendly for their then-five-year-old daughter. A perk was that their little girl was able to attend the same school in which Ashley worked, which made the transition for the family smoother. Another story of a move for a job that turned out to be a happy one for this family, even though it did not start out as such.

HAWAII

Fun Facts about Hawaii

- Hawaii's Haleakala Crater is the largest dormant volcano in the world, measuring seven miles across, two miles wide, and 2,600 feet deep.—*Wikipedia*

- Hawaii has the only royal palace in the United States. —*Fifty States and Fifty Fun Facts*

Kato, a physical education teacher, thinks of Las Vegas as home, even though change was hard for her when she moved from Hawaii to Las Vegas. She never thought she would stay here after college, but has made lifelong friends and continues to meet good people.

She is from a military family and lived in the Philippines for a time before moving to Hawaii, where she spent twelve years as a child. She grew up doing what kids do: exploring her surroundings, playing in the street until the lights came on, and, in her own words, "picking up boys." She had two aunts living in Las Vegas who needed assistance, and her family liked what they saw in Green Valley, specifically the schools. They never vacationed here; they just decided to make the move by packing up their belongings and getting on a plane.

Kato's dad retired from the navy, and they figured they would move to San Diego. However, they came to Las Vegas because of the aunts as well as the affordable housing compared to Hawaii. Kato has made a successful career as a teacher and would not think of moving away. In her own words, she says, "That would be drastic!"

IDAHO

Fun Facts about Idaho

- Idaho has the longest main street in America, thirty-three miles long, in Island Park. —*Fifty States and Fifty Fun Facts*

Sharon was an office manager and business owner living in Idaho for fifteen years. She never vacationed in Las Vegas nor rented a place before moving here. Then her husband was offered a more challenging job, which he wanted to try. After they moved to Las Vegas, Sharon was able to complete education courses, allowing her to become a teacher. She was the elementary school librarian who had great travel experiences, which we often discussed and which she used to stimulate her teaching.

Asked what surprised Sharon about Las Vegas, she responded that she did not expect such "vitality" juxtaposed to a "small-town feel" of this city. She thinks that the city is very separate from the tourism end of the valley and has much more to offer than meets the eye. It is a very real place to live, work, and raise a family, despite its reputation as Sin City.

INDIANA

Fun Facts about Indiana

- The famous car race the Indy 500 made its name here.—
  Fifty States and Fifty Fun Facts

Another teacher story from the Midwest…**Angela** lived in Indiana
on and off for twenty-three years and worked at Purdue University
in student affairs. She never vacationed in Las Vegas but moved for
her husband's employment.

She loved the weather and diversity of the city so much that her
family followed her move from the Midwest. Angela said, "What
I like about Las Vegas is that it has a small-town feel." By that she
means that she has found people to be open minded and friendly
in their thinking.

I met Angela at Jacobson Elementary, where I supervised her.
At that time she was working on changing her status from substitute teacher to permanent certification.

Regarding certification: Nevada does not make it easy for
teachers from out of state to get certified. It is as though the district and the state shoot themselves in the foot. I know that many
teachers have become discouraged by the process and changed
their mind about teaching here. This is a paradox for a city that
desperately needs good teachers. Great learning techniques from

other states can be brought to Las Vegas to improve the quality of education, yet roadblocks are put up to prevent that from happening. Retention of teachers has been a habitual problem as well. Many teachers leave after two or three years to return home to be with family or because they've become dissatisfied with the system. A sad commentary for education in Nevada.

KANSAS

Fun Facts about Kansas

- The world's largest concentration of boulders resides in Rock City, Kansas.—*Wikipedia*

Terri lived in a small Kansas town of three thousand people for thirty years. She had some odd jobs to help with college expenses, such as fast-food waitress, Kansas State University telephone operator, and executive secretary. She and her husband honeymooned and vacationed in Las Vegas three separate times. They actually drove around with a map, marking off places they would *not* live.

The couple moved to Las Vegas on their third anniversary, in 1991, to pursue teaching opportunities, which Terri did for many years. They love the weather but have mixed feelings about the move being a good decision for several reasons. Terri stated that people are somewhat unfriendly and uneducated, and the state doesn't value education. She feels somewhat unsafe as well.

The differences between growing up in a small town and living in a city like Las Vegas are many, and it took time to acclimate. She is still bothered by the blocked walls, the brown color of the desert, and the transient nature of people. She was used to more stability in her neighborhood in Kansas, unlike what she has experienced in Las Vegas. But waking up to sunshine every day is a real plus!

Even though Terri was concerned about the lack of focus on education and the value placed on it in Las Vegas, she spent many successful years teaching elementary school, and their son, Grant, received a fine education, participated in sports and student council, and was in the honors program. He is graduating from college next year with excellent career expectations. This proves again that there *are* some excellent educational opportunities of which families can avail themselves to set career paths for life.

KENTUCKY

Fun Facts about Kentucky

- The largest underground cave in the world is in Kentucky. The Mammoth Cave system runs for three hundred miles.—*Fifty States and Fifty Fun Facts*

Linda, a teacher in Clark County School District, came to Las Vegas after living in her home state of Kentucky for twenty-seven years. There she worked in the restaurant business and security, as well as owning a subcontracting printing company.

Her father lived and worked in California until he lost his business. He owned a condominium in Las Vegas where he vacationed, and that enabled him to move to Vegas. Linda has family living in other parts of Nevada: Elko, Carson City, and Pahrump. She visited these Nevada cities with her dad as a young child, "remembering the lights of the downtown city."

Linda moved to Northern Nevada and worked as a substitute teacher, but her father convinced her to come to Las Vegas and apply to the school district, where she was hired and still works. Initially, she was excited to be in Las Vegas. However, that wore off because she missed the friendliness of her home state. Linda says, "Las Vegas has a transient population, making it difficult to make lasting friendships. I miss knowing my neighbors."

MICHIGAN

Fun Facts about Michigan

- Muskegon, Michigan, is home to "snurfing," an early version of snowboarding.—*Fifteen Things You Might Not Know about Michigan*

Chelsea spent her childhood and college years in Michigan and has lived in Las Vegas now for over ten years. She had a childhood friend who moved to Las Vegas right after high school as a result of her father getting a job here. Chelsea came out for a week one summer to visit and stayed with her friend to determine whether she would like living here.

Chelsea is a very independent person and knew she wanted to get away from Michigan, just for a change. She stated, "Michigan gets pretty cold and very gloomy, but summers are beautiful." The cold weather in Michigan was a deterrent. However, Las Vegas never crossed her mind, but California and Florida did. She moved here because her father felt comfortable sending her someplace where there was a trusted friend who had a parent living here. Aside from this family, she moved without knowing a single other person!

Her experiences in Las Vegas have been positive, although when she first moved here, she experienced panic/anxiety attacks, which a doctor attributed to Chelsea being away from her family.

Luckily, she overcame them. Now she loves the sun, and her family visits often. Actually, her parents also came to love Las Vegas so much, they purchased a home here, in which Chelsea lives. She has found fulfillment in her teaching career with Clark County School District.

Diversity was what surprised Chelsea about Las Vegas, as she'd grown up in a small town without much of it. In 2014 Chelsea wrote that her only disappointment was that there were no major teams in Las Vegas…See how this town has changed?

MISSOURI

Fun Facts about Missouri

- At 630 feet, Missouri's Gateway Arch in St. Louis is the tallest stainless-steel monument in the world.—*Wikipedia*

Shelley was substitute teacher living in Missouri for seven years when her then husband was transferred to Las Vegas to open and manage a store. At that time most of her family lived here, and she visited often. She was especially close to her brother, with whom she maintains a very special relationship. She viewed moving to Las Vegas as a great decision twenty-three years ago, and she says, "I was surprised at how easily I made friends, finding it a wonderful place to live."

She was able to become certified to teach and has done so for over twenty years, almost all of them at Treem Elementary, which is where we met. She has been a very successful and beloved third grade teacher who not only successfully taught hundreds of students in her career but also mentored many student teachers from UNLV. Shelley and her boyfriend, Rick, enjoy retirement in their chosen city. Traveling is made easy for them because Shelley's son works for the airlines.

MINNESOTA

Fun Facts about Minnesota

- Minnesota is nicknamed "the Land of Ten Thousand Lakes." It has at least 11,842 lakes of ten acres or more. —*Fun Facts about Minnesota*

- Bob Dylan, F. Scott Fitzgerald, and Judy Garland are famous Minnesotans.—*Lynn Rosenberg*

As a personal care attendant for children with special needs, **Ashton** came to Las Vegas fifteen years ago after living in Minnesota for twenty-three years. He said, "School districts in Minnesota were facing budget cuts and closing, so I knew I would not get a job for several years if I stayed there. I had an interview with a recruiter for Clark County School District and got hired as a teacher." He only visited Las Vegas twice before moving here, but he attended a job fair and had two interviews, one in Las Vegas and the other in Alaska. He made up his mind that whichever district came through was his ticket out of Minnesota. On a personal note, he is an African American who married a white woman in Las Vegas. He told this writer that his biracial marriage would not have been so accepted in Minnesota as it is in Las Vegas, the city of diversity!

The opportunity to work for a large school district served him well, enabling him to move up from substitute teacher to new teacher mentor and school counselor. He has been surprised (as most people are) that there is more to this city than the strip.

MONTANA

Fun Facts about Montana

- The sedimentary rocks in Montana's Glacier National Park are the best preserved in the world and are believed to be 1.6 billion years old.—*Wikipedia*

Shelby's twin sister moved to Las Vegas to pursue a job as a technical theater major, figuring there would be more career opportunities here than in her small town in Montana. Shelby came to Las Vegas with her parents to help secure a place for her twin to live. She and her sibling had lots of fun riding the roller coaster and traveling the strip as tourists, and they gradually became sold on Las Vegas as a real place to live.

Shelby never thought she'd live here. She wanted a place with mountains and green grass everywhere. She never wanted to live in the southwestern part of the United States either. However, she decided to move here as a music major because, as she put it, "Most people tend to stay in one place in Montana." She was from a town of two thousand and was surprised at how huge Las Vegas was. Shelby joked, "There are more people than that in one block here!" Las Vegas has been a good place for both sisters to pursue their creative talents. Shelby's sister works in theater, and Shelby teaches music to elementary students and embraced the Smith Center

Disney Curriculum for schools. Shelby showed great talent directing several musical productions.

OKLAHOMA/WYOMING

Fun Facts about Oklahoma

- The "state meal" of Oklahoma is fried okra, squash, cornbread, barbecue pork, biscuits, sausage and gravy, grits, corn, strawberries, chicken fried steak, pecan pie, and black-eyed peas.—*Interesting Facts about Oklahoma*

Mary attended eleven different elementary schools, and by the time she entered sixth grade, her mother refused to move around Oklahoma any more. "I was born in Oklahoma, where my dad was an oil field rig worker, and we felt about as welcome as gypsies or migrant workers except for the fact that we brought money to the economy," said Mary.

The family settled in rural Wyoming, where she attended college and decided to pursue a career in geology. She was advised against it because a professor told her she would probably be unemployed for half of her life! She took his advice and returned to Oklahoma to finish college. An accident in her senior year caused her to return to her parents' home in Wyoming. She graduated from college there.

Teaching jobs were scarce in Wyoming, and she had to be prepared to teach several subjects and coach as well. She came to Las Vegas to teach sixth grade. Vegas, the glitzy city, was the complete antithesis of the small rural towns in Oklahoma and Wyoming that she kept crisscrossing during her childhood and early adulthood.

Eyvonne said, "I decided to elope here." She came to Las Vegas in 1970 from Oklahoma because she liked the weather and the laid-back atmosphere, and she decided to stay after her wedding. She got a job teaching sixth grade and loved spending time riding dirt bikes in the desert, water skiing with and without a wet suit in Lake Mead, and snow skiing at Mount Charleston in the winter. She also skied at resorts in Colorado and Utah.

Even after her divorce, she decided to stay, because by that time she had many friends who enjoyed the same activities she did. She was able to continue to participate in sports that she loved here and all over the world. She has enjoyed fifty years of living in Las Vegas, and as of this writing, she still enjoys her work as an elementary resource room teacher.

SOUTH DAKOTA

Fun Facts about South Dakota

- South Dakota is the home to the famous Mount Rushmore, the sculpture by Gutzon Borglum, of Thomas Jefferson, Theodore Roosevelt, Abraham Lincoln, and George Washington.—*Lynn Rosenberg*

MOUNT RUSHMORE, SOUTH DAKOTA

Dana had a variety of jobs when she lived in the northeastern part of South Dakota for twelve years. She was a carhop, cook, and counter server at the Tastee Treat Drive-In.

After her parents' divorce, Dana stayed with her dad and his new family in Las Vegas in 1978 and attended UNLV, where she met friends and her husband as well as earning a teaching degree. She's lived in Las Vegas since 1981.

Dana stated, "I am amazed how fast Las Vegas has grown since I moved here, and I'm thrilled with my friends and acquaintances." She is a librarian in an elementary school in Clark County, where she has found her niche. She loves books and enjoys teaching research skills to her students to prepare them for accessing resources for their education and avocations.

TEXAS

Fun Facts about Texas

- NASA in Houston is the headquarters for all piloted US space projects.—*Fifty States and Fifty Fun Facts*

Brett, a physical education teacher for Clark County School District, came to Las Vegas almost twenty years ago for the first time to attend his sister's wedding. He liked it and interviewed at Embassy Suites that weekend for a teaching job. He decided that the combined package of good pay, retirement benefits, and health insurance all were more favorable than his present job of teaching in Texas.

His wife, **Lori**, is a principal of an elementary school in the district. Therefore, the couple benefits from time off from work, sharing common school holidays and vacations, permitting them to travel and spend time as a family.

Brett and Lori have raised three children in Las Vegas and made many friends. Brett can play sports and teach young people to love athletics and physical fitness while earning a living. He benefits from the four-hour proximity to surfing and skiing.

Olga M. lived in Texas for twenty years and worked as waitress in a bar and deli while she was attending college. She had no family in Las Vegas, yet she moved to the city thirty-five years ago after she interviewed and got a job with EG&G/EM as an electronic technician. She said that her work at first was awful and her closest family member was in Barstow, California. She planned on staying in Las Vegas for only three years; however, many of her coworkers were from South Texas, so they made her feel at home in Las Vegas, and her sister moved here after Olga did, so she was not so lonely.

She stated, "I quit a great-paying job to go back to my first goal of being a teacher." This surprised even her!

Olga is an elementary teacher in Clark County School District, combining classroom teaching with her knowledge of technology, which has proven quite helpful to her colleagues and students. When I met Olga at Jacobson Elementary School, I was told, "Anything you need regarding computers, you can ask Olga!"

Her students leave her classroom at the end of the year having learned how to navigate programs and spreadsheets and to do projects utilizing PowerPoint. This gives them an advantage over other students as well as helping them with life skills needed for the future.

UTAH

Fun Facts about Utah

- Utah's Rainbow Bridge is the world's largest natural bridge, at 290 feet tall and 275 feet long.—*Wikipedia*

Bonnie moved to Las Vegas over twenty years ago because her husband's job transferred him here. She grew up in the small farming town of Antimony, Utah, and lived there for eighteen years.

Bonnie likes living here and feels the move was a good decision because of the warm weather compared to the cold of Utah. The contrast between a small town and the big city of Las Vegas is appealing to her because, she stated, "Las Vegas is a twenty-four-hour city where one can get fast food or shop any time of day or night." Bonnie also loves the proximity to the national parks, having become used to the beauty of the red rocks in her home state. She did not have to give that up when they moved to Las Vegas.

Bonnie found her calling in teaching for the school district. When I met her, she was part of a successful team of first grade teachers.

The following are a few excerpts from letters written to some of the educators featured in this book from students and parents whom they served well.

"You inspired me a lot, and you understood all that I was going through. You taught me how to write, and because of you, I won a poetry contest. I also let out my feelings to you, and I'd like you to know that I cannot do that with anyone else. I'd like to say thank you for all you have done for me. I will always remember you and keep you in my heart forever."
—A. B., a fifth grade student

"You could be of great help with J's move to Arizona, even though you weren't one of her teachers. As a principal, your unbelievable knowledge of children's learning styles would help her new teacher. You have been able to assess her needs and develop strategies far before I was able to as her parent. You took special interest in J. that goes above and beyond your position. There are no words to describe how I feel about your ability to communicate with parents; you can always find the positive. You will never be forgotten."
—D. L., parent of a third grader

"You have been an inspirational mentor, sharing both personal and professional experiences. You've taught me organization, the importance of context, and compassion for the students' individual needs. Your constructive criticism was of great value and importance to me."
—R. B., student teacher

"Thank you for answering the call to be a teacher and the enduring impression you've made in the lives you have touched. You look

beyond each child's face and inside their souls. Your contributions are immeasurable, and you improve our world."
—C. and D., third grade parents

"I do not have the words to thank you for all you have done for M. this year. He has truly flourished under your tutelage. It has been a wondrous year for him. It was a privilege to share him with you."
—J. H., third grade parent

"It has always been paramount to us that the people that surround our children are examples we want them to emulate. You are one of those people. Your loving kindness for every child, not just ours, is an example of the character you portray to our children each day."
—A. and M., third grade parents

"Thank you for all the travel presentations you showed us. They gave me motivation to travel the world when I'm older. It must have taken lots of energy to create them."
—G. S., middle school student

"I enjoyed your presentations on your travels so much, especially telling us the religious importance of Israel. I really want to see the Jewish Children's Memorial there, and the Amazon jungles in South America, and the zodiac boats in Antarctica."
—J., Eighth grader

"I was in your geography class last year, and I just wanted to say thank you for all you did for me. I know I wasn't the best student, but you believed in me, and I wanted to thank you for that."
—B. L. P., eighth grader

"I hope that you read this letter and write back. I think it would be neat to hear from a teacher who has made a difference in my life. I may not have known it then, but now I realize what it took to teach me. As I read through the memory book, my eyes filled with tears. Not one other teacher took the time to put my writings in a book. You were an inspiring teacher."
—Fourth grade student

"You've given your students the confidence to believe that they can accomplish more than they thought possible. They have learned so much, and even more importantly, they love to learn. What a great way to start their long journey. I couldn't have asked for more. Thank you from the bottom of our hearts."
—First grade parents

"You are the magic that helped J. begin his 'chase.'"
—A first grade parent, referring to the book *Thank You, Mr. Falker*

"A teacher like you only comes along once in a lifetime, and only certain children get the privilege of experiencing how it feels to have a teacher who cares. I'm so happy to be one of those privileged children."
—Fourth grade student

IMMIGRANTS CAME TOO

Argentina

Australia

England

Egypt

Germany

Mexico

Philippines

South Africa

South Vietnam

Yugoslavia/Serbia

THE WORLD

ARGENTINA/NORTH DAKOTA

Fun Facts about Argentina

- Argentina is known as one of the most literate countries in the world and prides itself in producing highly literate citizens that can easily maneuver around and succeed in the global business world.—*Fifty Facts about Argentina*

Judy lived over thirty-five years in Argentina before emigrating to the United States over thirty years ago. She and her husband, who was a doctor, settled in Bismarck, North Dakota, and lived there for fifteen years before coming to Las Vegas twenty-one years ago. Judy worked as a teacher and Spanish translator. The couple vacationed here and followed her husband's parents, who moved to Las Vegas.

Judy's husband wanted to move here, but as with many stories told before, Judy did not. She was not very happy in the beginning of their time in Las Vegas, because it seemed as though people here were transient. She worked in her husband's medical office and helped as needed. "Living in North Dakota, my accent was an eyesore. In Las Vegas it was recognized everywhere," she said.

As years went on, Judy felt more of a fit with Las Vegas, and her accent, which was problematic in North Dakota, became recognizable to the diverse population of Las Vegas. That led to more significant friendships for the couple, which have sustained Judy since the passing of her husband nine months ago. She is happy that she met so many nice people in the last few years, and her opinion of living in Las Vegas has improved due to solid human connections! She also enjoys the restaurants and entertainment the city offers.

The diversity that defines Las Vegas was a definite plus to Judy, as it helped her integrate into the city with more ease than she had in North Dakota, which has a less varied population than Las Vegas.

"The melting pot New York used to be is now Las Vegas." That's what my friend Beth said when I told her I was writing a book about people coming to Las Vegas. I think many of my stories reflect the truth of this statement.

EGYPT

Fun Facts about Egypt

- Located at Giza, the Pyramid of Khufu is the largest pyramid in Egypt. Measuring 146.7 meters in height, it's one of the oldest historic sites that remain largely intact. This pyramid is also known as the Pyramid of Cheops.—*"67 Wonderful Facts about Egypt," Wonderful Wanderings*

When I attend a concert, I want to hear music favorites, but I also want to know a little (or a lot) about the artist. Well, that is just what I got when I listened to **Michelle Johnson** at Cabaret Jazz at the Smith Center on October 20, 2019.

The program was billed as all the songs from Carole King's *Tapestry* album—and that it was! Michelle cleverly wove her story of success through King's songs from this very iconic album from 1970. Johnson kept telling her stories as she led into each of the fifteen or so songs she sang. It was a very interesting technique, enabling the audience to know her as well as explain how she'd come to love music.

Johnson lived in New York until she was four years old. It was then that her father, who worked at the United Nations, was transferred to Egypt, where Michelle spent her childhood and teenage years. She revealed that her high school graduation picture was taken in front of the pyramids at Giza! How many people can make that claim? She grew to love music after she won her first record album (*Black Sabbath*) in a raffle, and she played it until there were no grooves left. Comically, she likened herself to being a "Jewfrican," because she grew up loving music by Carole King and Barbra Streisand, had curly hair, and lived her early and later years in New York City.

Michelle attended Yale, as her parents wanted her to become a lawyer. However, her love for music as well as her talent grew in New Haven, where she changed majors and entered the Yale School of Music. This led her to connections and New York City after college. She did some recording and met some crazy characters, or, as she referred to them, "assholes," in her industry. This transitioned to the song "Slap Water Jack," about unsavory characters in New York who were dishonest and difficult to work with. Later, she was given the opportunity to sing with Gladys Knight, which was her dream, and that brought her to Las Vegas, where she was able to get steady work, initially at the Golden Nugget. Since then, Michelle has performed with many talented singers in Las Vegas and is a regular at the Smith Center. Ms. Johnson calls Las Vegas her home. She made the audience laugh when she joked that one of the great benefits of life in Las Vegas is that when you wake up in the morning, your car is still where you parked it. All the New Yorkers in the audience understood that reference!

The singer told several heartfelt stories throughout the ninety-minute concert. The most emotional story was the sad recounting of the death of her husband of seven years, Scott, from cancer. She told the audience that on his deathbed, he said how much he'd loved their lives together and felt he had been fulfilled. This led into their last conversation and the song "Will You Love Me Tomorrow," in which she shared her belief that love never dies and it follows you even when death takes a loved one. Trust me when I say there was not a dry eye in the house, including mine.

As part of her personal mantra, she espoused positivity, feeling beautiful about yourself, and taking chances to do something that motivates you yet you haven't tried. This led to the song "Beautiful," which is also the name of the Broadway show about Carole King's life. As a sidebar, I went to the ladies' room after the concert and was privy to a discussion by two women who both wanted to try singing in their sixties! Johnson apparently really got to the audience!

To finish off this great performance, Michelle showed a video of a new song she wrote called "I'm All In," about her commitment to singing and a tribute to Carole King. Afterward she took photos with her fans and provided the opportunity to sign up on her website for information on future events. She showed herself to be a real person with an honest story about how her career developed and brought her to Las Vegas, which made for a real connection to the audience.

As a footnote to this story, when I turned fifty, my dad threw me a beautiful birthday party at his country club here in Las Vegas. In a speech that I made thanking my family and friends for coming and adding to my life, I referenced this same *Tapestry* album as a metaphor for all the people who enriched my life and contributed to the woman I became. Each person was a thread in my tapestry and played a significant role in my development; to all of them I am grateful even today, twenty years later. My tapestry has only become fuller, richer, and deeper with each passing year because of the friends and family who continually add to it.

MICHELLE JOHNSON, PERFORMER.
PHOTOGRAPH BY ED FOSTER

GERMANY

POLAND

NEW JERSEY

LAS VEGAS

Fun Facts about Germany

- One -third of Germany is still covered in forests and woodlands.- *44 Fun and Interesting Facts about Germany*

Henry, who is known as a national treasure, just celebrated his one hundredth birthday. That's an amazing fact considering he is a Holocaust survivor who says he feels like seventy-five years old, not one hundred. He was interviewed for Holocaust Remembrance Day on April 20, 2020, by Rabbi Felipe Goodman on a Zoom chat because speaking to a packed congregation was not a possibility at this time due to the pandemic. I wrote his story from the oral interview he participated in.

Henry was born in Breslau, Germany, in 1920 and lived there until WWII broke out, with Germany invading one community at a time. His family moved to Katowice, Poland, which was on the border of Poland and Germany. In 1939, going to Russia was safer, so his mother and sister went first. Henry and his father were to follow, except that didn't happen because restrictions at that time forbade Jews from traveling. Both father and son were taken to Krakow and lived in a rented room with seven other people. Henry described the food being scarce and sickness rampant.

Each morning the men had to report to a labor camp, where they received a food stamp entitling them to a plate of watery soup and a crust of hard bread. As stories of other survivors corroborate, proving to a guard that one had a needed trade was something that saved many lives. So when an SS guard needed somebody to paint his apartment, Henry said that he was a great painter and that it was his trade. The truth was, he had never painted a day in his life, but he saw this as a lifeline.

Germans were always working with a plan to liquidate all the ghettos and would not let the Jews return to their families, housing them in a prison. Sadly, Henry never saw his mother again, and his father developed typhoid fever, which was common. Even though he recovered, sadly he was later killed. Henry was imprisoned in three concentration camps for a period of three years until 1945. His camp was referred to as the granite quarry, which housed fifty thousand people. He described walking with wooden shoes in the snow and bitter cold of the camps, where 70 percent of the prisoners did not survive. Fortunately, Henry was among those who did survive the horrors and atrocities of the Nazi regime. He saw the American jeeps roll into the camp on the glorious day of April 11, 1945, liberating the prisoners.

After liberation, he and his wife came to America in 1947 and lived in New Jersey, where Henry was a painter (for real) and a baker. He said that the hardest part of this life was trying to find some normalcy after all he had endured, because he didn't know what he was going to do until circumstances led him to his work and a real life.

After the life he had led in the camps, he knew that his mother had perished, but he still never knew the fate of his sister, and he thought about her every day, hoping that by some miracle she might be alive. That miracle came when he and his wife were invited to a wedding in New Jersey and a wedding in Montreal on the same day in November of 1960. They could not attend both events, and his wife suggested they stay in New Jersey and not make the drive to Montreal during the winter. However, Henry was more motivated to attend the wedding in Montreal, as the couple to be married there was closer to him. He sat at a table and started talking to a guest, and it was determined that the gentleman was from the same town in Germany where Henry was born. As the two men spoke, Henry asked the other man on a whim if he remembered his sister. Much to Henry's surprise, not only did the other guest know his sister, but he knew where she was living on Long Island!

Due to the fact that his sister had an unlisted phone number, Henry had a very hard time finding her until he begged the operator to help him, telling her his story and the need to find his sister. The operator complied, and Henry went to Long Island to find his sister, who ironically was packed and about to move to Las Vegas—of all places! Henry and his family followed her, and he has lived here since 1961, making a very meaningful life for himself, all along believing that once again, "Circumstances directed me!"

Henry has made an amazing contribution, along with about seventy-five other Holocaust survivors living in Las Vegas, to educating young people about the horrors of the Holocaust so they understand that it really happened and that an atrocity such as this should *never* happen again. These survivors have a common mission in warning young people that bullying and intolerance are the precursors of what happened so long ago to so many millions of people.

LONDON, ENGLAND

Fun Facts about London

- Numerous famous people have lived in London, including Karl Marx, Charles Darwin, Sylvia Plath, Charles Dickens, Jimi Hendrix, Wolfgang Amadeus Mozart, Florence Nightingale, and hundreds of others. Blue plaques now hang where these people lived.—*20 Facts That You Never Knew about London*

Robyn was born in Australia and lived there for twenty-four years before moving to London, England, where she lived for fifteen years. She and her husband, **Orest,** have lived in Las Vegas for thirty-seven years.

In the 1970s Robyn came to Las Vegas on a recreational vehicle vacation trip to visit the national parks. She thought Las Vegas was okay, but Robyn wasn't impressed. She could not believe it was the Entertainment Capital of the World. She found it to be colorful at night but boring during the day. Yet she has found over the years that there is plenty to do if you look for it.

She met her future husband, Orest, while vacationing in the Soviet Union and fell in love. He was working for EG&G in Las Vegas, supporting nuclear testing, while she was teaching in London. She really did not want to leave London nor her position.

However, she was able to get a job teaching in Las Vegas, whereas her future husband could not get a similar position in nuclear testing in London because there was no nuclear testing there. Therefore, Robyn was the one to move if they were to be together. Through her husband, Robyn met several Soviet government officials. She and Orest enjoyed taking the "anticapitalists" to have their picture taken with them in front of the display of one million dollars at Binion's Horseshoe Casino!

Arriving in Las Vegas brought with it some stress. She arrived at the airport with most of her belongings, only to find that Orest was not there, nor did she answer his phone. She was a bit scared because she had closed down her life in London, and she didn't know what she would do in a strange city in a strange country, knowing no one except Orest. Happily, he showed up an hour late (which turned out to be a typical habit of his).

Robyn says that the best thing about living in Las Vegas is that the city is attractive to so many people that many of her friends and family from Australia and the United Kingdom have come to visit. In addition, it is a great starting point for some wonderful national parks, such as Zion, Bryce, and the Grand Canyon.

What she thinks has changed about herself in her years in Las Vegas is that she used to keep people at arm's length as opposed to hugging all the time, which she found embarrassing when she first arrived. Additionally, she found signing off "with love" was something she rarely did, feeling that was reserved for special relationships. Today, those early habits have dissipated in favor of relaxed standards.

When asked about the worst thing about living in Las Vegas, Robyn answered, "The heat in the summer." She has become accustomed to that after so many years, and now what troubles her most is the attitude toward education. She continued, "When a cocktail waitress or a valet can earn more than a teacher, it becomes hard to convince students that education is important." It is true that facts like these are a disincentive to students working hard in school and furthering their education in college.

MEXICO

Fun Facts about Mexico

- Mexico is the eleventh-most populated country in the world, with around 117 million people (as of July 2012).

- Mexico is the fourteenth largest country by land area.

- There are thirty-one states in Mexico, as well as the capital city (Mexico City). —*Facts You Did Not Know about Mexico*

The story of **Rosa** is a typical yet very important story of why people flee Mexico. Rosa lived in Guadalajara for twenty-one years. It is the capital of the state of Jalisco, and it has a population of 1.5 million people. It is the fifth-most populous city in Mexico, famous for tequila and mariachi music.

She was a waitress and housekeeper in Mexico. Crime was not a real problem, but she wanted a better and safer life for her twins, Maria and Jose. Rosa left family in Mexico but had family here as well.

Initially Rosa did not like Las Vegas because the language was different for her, but she adjusted and has made a happy life for her family. Their twins were educated in Las Vegas and attended college in Reno. Maria became a speech pathologist, and Jose became a mechanical engineer. Rosa's husband, **Fernando**, was a painter and is now a landscaper, and Rosa runs a successful housekeeping business, helping with catering and parties as well. Rosa stated that she likes owning her own business, enjoys working with her staff of housekeepers, and feels good about serving her clients.

The only thing that came to mind when questioned about what she dislikes about living in Las Vegas was the summer heat. She is not alone with that. She says that the availability to purchase anything she wants separates her life here from her life in Mexico. She appreciates that greatly.

THE PHILIPPINES

Fun Facts about the Philippines

- The country is known for having its rich biodiversity as
  its main tourist attraction. Its beaches, heritage towns and
  monuments, mountains, rainforests, islands, and diving
  spots are among the country's most popular tourist destinations.—*Facts about the Philippine Culture*

Stories come from places you would not expect them to...

This winter I went for a simple medical test and started talking to the DMS (diagnostic medical sonographer) about questions
related to the procedure, which led to her training and then to
her story about coming to Las Vegas. This story had a surprising
ending.

Cecilia left Manila and came to this country to be with relatives.
Her family had a business selling medical equipment in Manila
and then in Tennessee, so she had a bit of a medical background,
in addition to training as a midwife. She came to Las Vegas from
Knoxville in 1994 on a vacation and met her future husband, who
was in the air force. Within a week of meeting him, he proposed.
According to custom, she had to go to counseling with him for

three months while courting. She was twenty-seven at the time but was respectful of her family's wishes.

With her medical background in Manila, Cecilia took courses at UNLV for two years as a DMS and now works for several cardiologists, doing imaging as well as working in a hospital administering sonograms. This discussion continued during my procedure, and we talked about school—only to find out that her five-year-old daughter, Joanna, had attended my elementary school that year as a kindergartner! What are the chances of that?

Cecilia said that living was safe in Manila because of the president, but she likes the life she has here and the opportunity for advancement. Education is important to her. She mentioned that her nineteen-year-old son attends UNLV. Her husband, now ex-military, provides security for one of the hotels. This led to a conversation about concern for safety in the world today.

As a sidebar, Clark County School District employs many teachers (especially in the field of special education) from the Philippines. Representatives of the school district travel there yearly to recruit. Many of these recruits come here to work, earning considerably more money than they do in the Philippines. They find happiness with their lives in Las Vegas and move here permanently.

POLAND

Fun Facts about Poland

- Popular Polish foods include mushroom barley soup, kielbasa and cabbage, veal meatballs with dill, and dried fruit compote, which is usually served at the end of Christmas Eve dinner. —*Facts and Food from Poland*

Anna and Andrzej lived their whole lives in Poland (with the exception of a four-year sojourn in Ireland) until their family was selected in the visa lottery in 2015 to move to the United States. Anna was an early childhood teacher and occupational therapist in their home country, and Andrzej was a computer systems administrator. Andrzej came to Las Vegas first because they had friends living here. He rented a condominium for a good price and renovated it to his liking before he brought his wife and child here. Their friends said that the real America is the West Coast. New York was a consideration for the family, but it was too expensive, and they figured the quick pace of New York was a little off-putting for new immigrants.

Anna says that they didn't have any real expectations for America. "It was a totally different world, and we were giving ourselves a chance." They figured that the worst-case scenario would be going back to Poland. However, they knew they had a solid work ethic, and they would be pushed to succeed more in America than in Poland.

The couple feels incredibly blessed to have met good people who have given them opportunities to do well in their respective work. Anna is an assistant preschool teacher, and Andrzej is a computer specialist for Clark County School District. Their six-year-old daughter learned English easily, and she is doing quite well in school. The kindness of the people was their surprise in moving to Las Vegas. They were helped to integrate into the school community. They are well liked, quite ambitious, and conscientious with their respective work ethic. We met when I was their supervisor at Gragson Elementary School.

Theirs is a real success story for a couple who gave Las Vegas a chance!

SOUTH AFRICA (CAPE TOWN)

Fun Facts about Cape Town

- The Cape Peninsula was originally known as the Cape of Storms. As a result of the terrible tempests that have been known to rock the Mother City's coastline, the Cape Peninsula was originally nicknamed the Cape of Storms by legendary explorer Bartholomew Dias. Later it became known as the Cape of Good Hope because it offered colonial powers the promise of a sea route to the east.—*Facts about Cape Town*

Noreen was born and lived in Cape Town for thirty years and moved to the United States in 1977. She lived in Texas, New York, and California before moving to Las Vegas fourteen years ago.

When her family left South Africa in 1977, they were only allowed to take $10,000 with them. All their assets were frozen, and they could only use their money if and when they returned to South Africa. They left with that amount of money and fifty-four boxes of household things.

Her husband's job was in the manufacturing of contact lenses, which took them to several states before landing in Las Vegas. While enjoying life in California, Noreen obtained a real estate license. When her nephew offered her a job in that field in Las

Vegas, all she knew about Las Vegas was the desert heat and casinos, really nothing about the lifestyle. As fate would have it, her sister had moved to Las Vegas two years prior. Noreen decided it would be wonderful to live close to her sister for once.

Now she has lived in Las Vegas for fourteen years and absolutely loves everything about it: the best restaurants, blue skies daily, hiking, theater, and bearable traffic (compared to Los Angeles)! Noreen said, "I am so sorry I did not move here years before, especially being in the real estate market. Sorry that I did not invest grandly in real estate earlier. Las Vegas is vibrant, exciting, and just the most friendly town one could wish to live in."

Noreen says that the world needs to know exactly what this great city has to offer: wonderful neighborhoods, world-class entertainment, the finest restaurants, and so much more.

CAPE TOWN, SOUTH AFRICA

CHAPEL HILL, <u>NORTH CAROLINA</u>
RENO, NEVADA
SAN FRANCISCO, CALIFORNIA
BEVERLY HILLS, CALIFORNIA
AND FINALLY LAS VEGAS

Fun Facts about North Carolina

- Virginia Dare was the first English child born in America on Roanoke Island in 1587.—*Fifty States and Fifty Fun Facts*

When **Charlene**'s husband, a physician, sold his practice to a big conglomerate in Beverly Hills, the couple needed to relocate so as not to violate his noncompete clause. As he was licensed to practice in Nevada, Las Vegas was the logical choice. As Charlene stated, not only was she not excited to move here, she thought Las Vegas was the "armpit" of the nation! She was really enjoying their life in Beverly Hills at the time they decided to move, because so many of her South African friends had settled there. Having lived in many places due to Dr. **Geoffrey**'s work, and feeling friendships in these places were sorely lacking, Las Vegas was the last place Charlene wanted to live.

So homesick was she that when they first moved here in 1997, she would drive to Los Angeles every other week to get her fix and keep up with the life and friends she had in Beverly Hills.

Charlene was told that people were both really nice and helpful in Las Vegas, and slowly these qualities began to emerge to her. After about six months, she stopped driving to LA, where she'd begun to notice the traffic was a nightmare, and many areas looked old and dirty compared to the freshness of Las Vegas. She questioned why she was going to LA so frequently and started to enjoy Las Vegas: the best restaurants, up-to-date fashion, moderate traffic situations, and wonderful modern homes—the best that America has to offer!

Charlene is involved in many charities and the promotion of theater groups, as well as acting. Charlene summed up their lives here and said, "Life is good here—really good! There are times I think we should have moved here earlier."

SOUTH VIETNAM

Fun Facts about South Vietnam

- Vietnamese boat people, also known simply as "boat people," were refugees who fled Vietnam by boat and ship following the end of the Vietnam War in 1975. This migration was at its highest in 1978 and 1979 but continued through the early 1990s.—*Wikipedia*

- Large-scale immigration from Vietnam to the United States began at the end of the Vietnam War, when the fall of Saigon in 1975 led to the US-sponsored evacuation of an estimated 125,000 Vietnamese refugees. As the humanitarian crisis and displacement of people in the Indochina region (Vietnam, Cambodia, and Laos) intensified, more refugees and their families were admitted to the United States. The Vietnamese immigrant population has grown significantly since then, roughly doubling every decade between 1980 and 2000, and then increasing 26 percent in the 2000s. In 2017 more than 1.3 million Vietnamese resided in the United States, accounting for 3 percent of the nation's 44.5 million immigrants and representing the sixth-largest foreign-born group in the country. —*Wikipedia*

The writer's nail technician, **Mai** (a.k.a. Crissi in the shop), was one of the many refugee stories. She left Saigon in 1980 because her family could not earn a living farming nor selling coffee. Her father was in the navy. After the end of the Vietnam War, the Communists made living in South Vietnam impossible, not allowing citizens to keep possessions nor earn a decent wage. Mai came over by boat. She described it as a small craft with fifty people on board. She traveled from South Vietnam to Thailand. There she spent two months in a refugee camp. Then she journeyed to the Philippines for six months, then California for ten years, and later lived in St. Louis in 2003. She finally made her home Las Vegas in 2004, where she and her husband could make a living and live more cheaply than in California.

She feels comfortable and safe here. It took her ten years to return to Saigon to visit family, and she was quite nervous that she would be detained there. She said she kept her mouth closed, concerned about saying the wrong thing. She said, "The fear of the Communists is real, and their behavior quite unpredictable, and you don't know what they would do." She described traveling by boat with poor conditions and lots of other refugees as a grueling experience.

In her own words, Mai related the horror of the boat ride to freedom:

"We were led to the boat on foot from our village when we were told it was time to leave. You never knew exactly when it would happen. The payment was in gold and jeweled trinkets. The boat held about fifty people, and I went with just my husband in 1983. We were on this boat for one full day and night with no food, and just enough water to wet our lips. We were fortunate to arrive safely in Thailand, where we stayed in a refugee camp for two months, learning English and how to manage appliances and skills needed to navigate our new life in the US. Some were not so lucky to reach the land. Women were raped, jewelry taken, and the women were thrown overboard. I kept my head down most of the time, afraid of what I might see. The next stop was Manila, where we stayed for a few months, again learning the tools we would need to live in America. They tested us on our language ability and life skills learned in the camps. Only when we passed these tests could we leave the camps. We headed for Los Angeles—the America we were waiting for."

After many years in Las Vegas, Mai has found her grounding here and works with other Vietnamese people with similar stories. Over two hundred thousand Southeast Asians live in Las Vegas. Even in the safety net of living in the United States for over thirty years, Mai has bad dreams. She told me told me that several times a year, she wakes up in the morning in a panic. Often she dreams that she is still in Vietnam and can't escape. It takes a few moments for her to realize it is only a dream, yet it frightens her each time.

Mai lived in several places in the United States, but she feels the most comfortable and happy in Las Vegas because of the beautiful weather and open air and spaces, which she did not have elsewhere.

Both her mother and grandmother had ten children each. Their children married and had children of their own. When she gets together in California with them, they have to take a room in a hotel because their family numbers close to five hundred!

These stories have been heard before about refugees from Southeast Asia after the Vietnam War. However, listening to Mai's story of her journey personalized this experience for this writer. I am grateful that my family never had to endure such hardships. The Vietnamese community in Las Vegas has found safety and security for themselves and their loved ones.

TORONTO, CANADA

Fun Facts about Toronto

- Analysts have listed Toronto as the most livable city in the world after Brisbane, Sydney, and Vienna.—*Cool Facts about Toronto*

Carole lived in Toronto for forty-nine years before relocating to Las Vegas over twenty-five years ago. She was a dental hygienist and then owned a business selling homemade taffy and nuts, creating gift baskets to order. Her husband, **Maurice**, grew up in Zimbabwe and attended medical school in Cape Town. He had a cousin who set him up with a position in Toronto, practicing medicine as a thoracic surgeon. The couple met on a blind date in Toronto, married, and lived there many years before making the move to Las Vegas, even though in 1960 it seemed like the least likely of destinations.

Carole and Maurice came to Las Vegas with some family members then on a junket. Maurice practiced craps for months before the trip, allocating a great deal of time each day to playing. The men went to the casinos, and the women shopped. Maurice lost both his money and his pride and vowed never to come back—until he had a great opportunity to join a medical practice in his field, where he ended up working for over nineteen years. Their family was amazed and shocked when Carole and Maurice announced they were moving to Las Vegas. However, she felt, "Moses was leading us into the desert."

After moving here, Carole did volunteer work in the community, and then became a Realtor. This enabled her to meet many people who became her network of friends, especially through the JCC (Jewish Community Center, now known as Jewish Nevada). The couple have never been disappointed living here and love the relationships they made. She said, "When you love what you do, you are fulfilling your destiny." Carole continued praising their lives in Las Vegas by touting the great weather and the good vibe that she feels defines Las Vegas. The couple enjoys watching the arts grow in Las Vegas with the kinds of programs and theater opportunities as were available in Toronto.

Other benefits about living in Las Vegas are that many people come to visit because there is so much to do. Often, she said, "I can't change the sheets and towels fast enough!" The couple has a great level of comfort looking out each morning at the view of the golf course from their window. "To succeed here here you need inspiration", said Carole, "which is easy in this growing city created from human initiative."

She has become more respectful of herself and has come to a comfortable place in life throughout her years living in Las Vegas. She also shared that while Maurice was practicing medicine, she had great connections to all the doctors in Vegas; since he has retired, those connections have not been as easy to come by.

Carole described an exciting experience meeting and kissing David Copperfield, the world-famous magician, when she was selected from the audience to do a trick. His trick was amazing, and it was so real that people asked her if she was a "plant" as she was leaving the theater!

It is not a surprise that even though the couple misses their family in Vancouver, they have no intentions of ever leaving Las Vegas.

This is a story about newbies Elisa and Ryan, who came to Las Vegas only six months ago from Toronto.

Elisa was an elementary school teacher for sixteen years in Canada. Ryan was an event and festival planner, which is what brought them to Las Vegas. He is the director of events and entertainment for Area 15. Ryan had been in charge of dance work events in New York and Barbados.

The couple had been to Las Vegas about eight times, always during the month of August, because Ryan took his DJs here as a stop during the World Electronic Event in Canada. The couple was always impressed with the weather and blue skies compared to Toronto's weather. It bodes well for Elisa to be impressed by weather in Las Vegas in August. To those of us who live here, we know that is not usually a selling point! They are pleased with their large and spacious home compared to their small condominium in Canada, which was the same price as their lovely home here.

Elisa and Ryan have eight-year-old twin boys, who attend a neighborhood public school. Elisa's love of education encourages her to volunteer in their school, and she has seen how our educational system works. She mentioned that the Ontario schools are in disarray, yet their kindergarten program combines play, socialization, and reading with a great balance.

Elisa stated that what surprised her the most about life in Las Vegas was that the people are very friendly, helpful, and nice. She indicated that she did not expect that. She thoughtfully added, "Maybe that is because many people we meet are in the service industry and are expected to be friendly." Even though she has met friendly people, one disappointment she mentioned was that kids don't play in the street, and she has not met many of her neighbors yet. She is not getting a "welcome vibe."

When questioned about a lesson she has learned living in Las Vegas, she responded, "Beware of safety." She realizes some areas should be approached with caution.

Hailing from Canada, where the Toronto Maple Leafs are a huge draw, she has been pleased that Las Vegas has embraced the Golden Knights in such a grand manner, with bumper stickers, game attendance, sportswear, and excitement for the team. She said, "It brings people together in such a positive way." Even her sons have become caught up in Golden Knight fever. Elisa and Ryan sat next to the lead investor of the Golden Knights, William Foley, at a recent game.

Elisa indicated that the family is taking better care of their health since moving to Las Vegas and spending more time together. She is an active tennis player and an advocate for physical fitness for all her family. Even in the short time Elisa and Ryan have lived in Las Vegas, she said that she would find it difficult to leave their beautiful home and great weather to move back to a condo in Toronto.

YUGOSLAVIA/SERBIA

Americans struggle to understand the complicated breakup of Yugoslavia, especially when visiting countries that have risen from its ashes, such as Croatia, Slovenia, Macedonia, and Bosnia-Herzegovina. Talking to the locals can make it even more confusing. Everyone in the former Yugoslavia seems to have a slightly different version of events, and mildly plausible (but specious) conspiracy theories run rampant. A very wise Bosniak once told me, "Listen to all three sides—Muslim, Serb, and Croat. Then decide for yourself what you think."—*Cameron Hewitt*

Misha is his name in the United States, Misa in Serbia. He was born in Tripoli, Libya, but moved to Yugoslavia (now Serbia) when he was two years old and lived there until he was eighteen. Misha finished high school and then served in the Yugoslavian army for one year.

Misha was an athlete scouted for tennis, which originally took him to college on an athletic scholarship in Tennessee. After two years his grant ran out and he was given the opportunity to come to Las Vegas, attend UNLV, and play tennis for the school team on scholarship. He was grateful for the continued opportunity to receive an education in the United States and the ability to play a sport he loved and in which he excelled. However, his plan never included staying in the States. He intended to return to Serbia. He did not want to be separated from his close family.

In Misha's own words, "As I was here, Vegas grew on me. It felt like home being here. In the late 1980s, my country was going through civil wars, and being a part of the American lifestyle of freedom made me feel safe." In addition, Misha stated that he was able to "grow to be his own person" each day. For him that meant making his own choices, both good and bad ones. He laughed and said that he worked on correcting the bad ones. He married out of convenience, but that didn't last. For years he was single, but now he has a loving wife and a solid marriage.

This tennis pro has found his place in Las Vegas. He heads a program at a tennis club, allowing him to play a sport he loves and teach others to appreciate and excel at it daily. The weather is a plus, giving him "energy to feel the openness of the desert." He told me that even when he leaves Las Vegas, as he returns home, his appreciation and love for the city envelop him. He said, "I can't really explain it." Yet as I looked at his face, he just did!

ACKNOWEDGEMENTS

The idea for this book came from all of the people who patiently spoke to me and wrote their stories for me to enhance. Without these real-life stories, there would be no book. Thank you to all of my subjects. Their stories all follow lines of taking chances in a city of gamblers.

I use the metaphor of a tapestry often from Carole King's album and song by the same name to acknowledge that all of the cooperative people along this journey made this happen. I wove their stories of how they arrived in Las Vegas, and I learned so much about places they left. I thank them for their candor and encouragement to me about writing this book.

On a personal level, my family, which is full of creative types on both sides, played a role in helping me fulfill my dream. My brother, Gary Goldstein, a screenwriter, was my "colleague" along the way to answer my many questions and listen to my work. The Kaplan family (Mark, Yvette, and Randall) happily created artwork. The image on the cover was copyrighted by Thomas Wolf (www.foto-tw.de, CC BY-SA 3.0) and reformatted by Mark Kaplan. My friend Sara Lopez drew several of the sketches that further define the stories.

Much appreciation is given to the *Las Vegas Review Journal* for kindly granting me permission to use the articles cited in my book. In addition, thank you to Diane Taylor for granting permission to exerpt her articles on Ed Foster, "Photographer Ed Foster Tells the

Stories," and Louise Unell, "Louise Unell: Volunteerism a Result of Cancer." Appreciation to Neal Portnoy for granting me permission to use his whimsical sketch of Ed Foster in the article. Thanks to Joan Peck for allowing me to use excerpts of her wonderful stories and using her article on Judith August "Judith August and the Magic of Serendipity."

As I was seriously writing the book, I took a class through UNLV/OLLI called Writers' Critique with other writers and a teacher, Richard Kram, who helped me to better clarify my ideas. They helped me question certain aspects of my writing. Additionally, my dear friend Kathe Brener did a thorough proof-read of my work, giving me many suggestions.

I thank the patient and talented people at Palmetto Publishing Group for guiding me through all the steps needed to publish *50 States, 50 Stories.*

I appreciate my patient husband, Ron, for sharing his computer, desk, and most importantly his support for my book. He was my cheerleader all the way.

And lastly, I must thank my dad, who moved to Las Vegas in 1994 when I thought it was unheard of to move here, yet we followed five years later, never thinking we'd live here…

ABOUT THE AUTHOR

Lynn S. Rosenberg (nee Goldstein) and her husband, Ron, have lived in Las Vegas for over twenty years. She grew up and lived in Long Island, New York. She attended the State University at Cortland in upstate New York, where she majored in elementary education, and Hofstra University, where she earned two master's degrees, one in reading and one in administration.

She pretty much followed the mold of what her friends on Long Island did: came back after college, married, had two children, and taught school. Life changed when she and her second husband (her first husband, Gary, died in 1985) moved to Las Vegas after frequently visiting her dad, who had relocated to Las Vegas for business. In 1999 she was offered a job as an assistant principal, which inspired the couple to leave New York for Las Vegas, a place far different from her roots.

Lynn's career was spent in the field of education, as a teacher and then an administrator. It was all Lynn wanted to do from the time she was in fifth grade because of a wonderful teacher who inspired her to one day enter the profession. While raising her two sons, Jeffrey and David, Lynn taught the upper elementary grades, and when the boys were ready for college, she decided it was time for more of a challenge and earned a degree in administration. She believed that instead of reaching twenty-five students a year, she could inspire more children being a principal.

Working as an assistant principal in several schools in Las Vegas, Lynn met many teachers who hailed from different places. The idea for this book developed because each person she met had an interesting story about how they came to live in Las Vegas. She collected questionnaires over a five-year period, and then upon her retirement, she decided it was time to write their stories.

She loves living in Las Vegas and enjoys exercising outdoors, playing tennis, biking, hiking Red Rock Canyon, and visiting her six grandchildren in Tennessee and California. The Rosenbergs have traveled extensively over the years to Hawaii, the Canadian Rockies, Alaska, Italy, Spain, France, Iceland, the national parks, and most recently Australia and New Zealand.

It is her hope that all her readers delight in these stories and, not surprisingly, find themselves!